Donated by

Pinehurst Garden Club

2005

Growing a Beautiful Garden

A Landscape Guide for the Coastal Carolinas

Growing a Beautiful Garden

A Landscape Guide for the Coastal Carolinas

By Henry Rehder, Jr.

photography by Freda H. Wilkins

Banks Channel Books
Wilmington, North Carolina

Edited by: Barbara Sullivan
Cover photography and interior photography except as otherwise noted: Freda H. Wilkins
Cover design and interior design: Jane Baldridge

Front cover: Garden at the home of James Moss Burns, Wilmington , N.C.

ISBN 0-9635967-9-9

Library of Congress Catalog Card Number 96-84203

Printed in Korea

First Banks Channel Books Printing: 1997
Second Printing: 1998
Third Printing: 2002

This book is dedicated to Barbara Gaines Rehder, who finds such beauty in the simplest of God's creations.

ACKNOWLEDGEMENTS

I owe a great deal of thanks to countless friends, fellow gardeners and horticulturists who have taught me so much about flowers, biology and the plant kingdom. The most valuable lesson seems to be that horticulture is not an exact science even though I think it should be. For every method of growing a plant, these folks seem to have a different way, using different methods and materials with better results. It is with gratitude that I thank them for their guidance and friendship.

The late Reid Lassiter took time and patience to teach me the ways of nature. Reid was a man who insisted on taking care of the landscape. He inspired me to be a common-sense gardener while seeking more complex reasons for the nature of plants and animals.

Ann Willard always opens her garden for me and is willing to teach new lessons and answer questions. Dr. Bruce Williams, one of the most colorful horticulturists I know, and his associate, David Vann Barkley keep an "open door" at their Extension Service offices. They are experts in plant taxonomy and pathology. John Cain, the manager of the New Hanover County Extension Service Arboretum is always quick to explain new techniques, plant acquisitions and recent developments.

The folks who work the gardens, the labs and greenhouses are significant contributors to my knowledge. Louisa Trigg Canady, Brec Connett, Kenny Kwiatek and Lester Wilson have helped immensely. Phil Ricks, The Master Gardeners Association and the Trustees of the Arboretum Foundation have been good friends.

Bob Townsend, Shirley Gilbert and Jon Evans support local horticulture and are always willing to expand the gardening format, yet they insist on quality reporting and accurate information.

I am indebted to the Trustees and staff of Oakdale Cemetery for the use of their grounds for research, especially Tom Sneeden who always greets me with a smile.

The support and friendship of Donn Ansell, Bill "J.J." Jefferay and the folks at WAAV Radio have extended many opportunities for which I am grateful.

I am particularly thankful to Les and Ann Turlington of Farmers Supply Company for their sponsorship, patience and help.

My father inspires me to grow things and provides greenhouse space, garden areas and constant advice. He, and my mother, who was a great horticulturist, have always been at the heart of my gardening experiences. Stan Rehder, my uncle, is a great naturalist. He supervised my growing at Fun City Farms and has taken me on countless field trips to study insectivorous plants.

I admire and thank Ellyn Bache, Freda Wilkins, Barbara Sullivan and Jane Baldridge for their amazing ability and professional skill.

The staff at the flower shop, Will Rehder Florist, keep the gears turning when I am not able. Tom Cheatham and Jay Lee have guided me through the maze of computer skills, and I say a large thanks to Eric Higgins for coining the phrase "Dr. Plant."

Any effort in the garden requires support of some type, and for me, it has been the intensive help of my associate, Laura Jean Houghton. Laura reviewed the pictures, studied the chapters, and through her research, made sure the culture was good and the botany correct. A horticulturist of the first order, she has been my best friend.

For the love and support of my wife, Diane, I will forever be thankful, especially when her encouragement meant so much during family crises and hurricanes.

I am eternally mindful and thankful for the inspiration from my daughter Johanna Howerton Rehder, who left us so suddenly, but who reaches from Heaven, and with a wonderful spirit of encouragement, smiles on the progress I know she sees from her place in Eternal Glory.

I thank my God, The Creator of The Universe, His Holy Spirit and my Saviour, Jesus Christ.

TABLE OF CONTENTS

INTRODUCTION

Gardening along the southeast coast can be an exciting hobby because of the uniqueness of the area. The growing season is almost 257 days long which means you can have flowers blooming in the garden nearly year 'round. In fact, the seasons merge so closely for flower and plant growers that we may see blooming plants crossing into seasons in which they are otherwise dormant. It gets confusing, especially for folks who move into this part of the country from colder areas. For example, our famous camellias begin flowering in November, persist through the winter months, and continue to bloom well into April. While they are in full production, the bulb plants, like daffodils and tulips, will appear in late winter, often completing their bloom period before winter officially ends. In the perennial flower beds, we may find chrysanthemums blooming in the spring which were at their peak the previous fall. In colder areas, garden mums may be treated as annuals. Canna lilies, a very popular plant throughout the country, are often taken out of the garden and stored for the winter, but here they bloom 'til frost and are simply left in the flower beds for the next season.

This crossing and merging of the seasons is one of the fascinating parts of gardening here, and folks are delighted to find themselves gardening as a hobby at odd times of the year like cool fall days and the balmy times of late winter. Even folks who have lived here for years are amazed at the unique growing season. They are often surprised at the number of plants that can be grown throughout the year. There is a wonderful excitement about raising plants and flowers as a twelve-month event.

This spirit of gardening is reflected throughout the region. From the tidewaters of North Carolina to the Georgia coast, the area boasts some splendid examples of well-established gardens that attract thousands of tourists every year. Along the southeast section of the North Carolina coast we have the famous Orton Plantation which has developed some superb hybrid azaleas and camellias from its colonial gardens. Airlie, the original Pembroke Jones Estate in Wilmington, N.C., combines old-world elegance with rural Southern charm. Here you will find small lanes and paths meandering through hundred year old azalea gardens and live oaks which have been tended by local gardeners for generations. Because this coastal part of the country was settled long before inland sections, the old gardens of the region have acquired great beauty with age.

The unique coastal environment, with its warm ocean breezes, steady amounts of rainfall and moderate temperatures, has created this gardening tradition. But it has also created a fair amount of challenge. The heat of the summer can easily stall active plants, throwing them into dormancy. Some insects are known only in this area — like ground pearl, a pest that feeds on the roots of centipedegrass. Petal blight, a spring fungal disease, seriously diminishes the blooming period of some azaleas, and our soils can be extremely acidic and lacking in humus. The hurricane season threatens gardens at the peak of their growing season, and ocean storms can send salt spray miles inland.

Our wonderful growing environment, coupled with our unique obstacles, makes it easy to understand why so many homeowners want and need good advice. This is true both for locals and the many folks who move into this area from other parts of the country and are not familiar with the region's climate.

For perhaps the first time, this guide presents a step-by-step, month-by-month plan that organizes garden tasks on a simple basis. It takes into consideration many of the variables that affect growing plants in our local conditions. The section for each species gives more detail on general cultivation, some facts about the plant which will help you decide on specific varieties and ideas for using the plant to its full advantage. The initial parts of the book deal with how to choose a plant, where to plant it and general cultivation requirements. All of this information is tailored for use in the coastal Carolinas.

Though the book doesn't include all of the plants that can be grown here, and certainly not all the countless cultivated varieties, it does outline some of the most popular. These are the plants that have made so many local gardens famous, not only for their ease in growing, but for their stately beauty, hardiness, resistance to pests and finally, their magnificence in age. Some selections are revivals of old classics, some are new hybrids. Many have been chosen for their popularity, some for pure serendipity.

From even a brief glance at the plant listings, it will be obvious that I have a bias toward ornamental shrubs. I've included more of these garden classics and fewer trees than you might find in other gardening books. There's a reason for this. Trees—especially the legendary Southern beauties like the magnolia and the dogwood—provide the essential structure, backdrop and canopy in any garden. But it is the fascinating variety of ornamentals with all their potential for form, texture and color that will really make your garden distinctive and beautiful.

Following the guide step-by-step will not guarantee success in your flower garden or landscape. But it may help you anticipate some of the situations which can come up over the course of the growing season. If you are aware of those things, you may be able to take advantage of the good influences and and lessen the impact of the bad.

My hope is that as you grow these plants for your pleasure, you might just accomplish a beautiful garden that is fun to raise and acquires distinctive character with age.

CHAPTER ONE

Choosing Your Plants

Color and Bloom Habit

We are blessed here in the coastal area with a long growing season. Our closeness to the Gulf Stream, the long summer and fall seasons, and the quick spring start-up provide a remarkable climate for growing plants of great character over a long period of time. When you select plants, aim for color, texture and variety in all twelve months. This will be easy to do because garden centers and nurseries usually have plenty of choices all year. They capitalize on our long season and you should, too. In the early spring you can choose from a large selection of early-flowering fruit trees like the Bradford pears, flowering cherries, and plum trees. In mid-spring, you'll find plenty of azaleas. As summer approaches, the nurseries will feature an old-South favorite, the crape myrtle, and mid-summer offers hydrangeas and daylilies. Summer is also an ideal time to purchase perennials for your color garden. The fall will bring the sasanquas and winter the camellias. You'll not be disappointed if you grow plants for year-round appeal.

Although there are many things to consider, the primary concern of most homeowners and gardeners is often the color of the plant and its bloom. It's always best to see the plant at the nursery or garden center when it is flowering so you can be sure the color is what you want. Nothing can be more disappointing than to expect a shrub to bloom a deep pink and then to find, after waiting a full season, that the flower is actually red. Pictures, of course, are good guides, as are descriptions — but to be exact, it's always best to purchase your plant when it is in full bloom.

It's also important to learn the bloom style and habit before you buy. Some flowering plants give lots of color quickly, the blooms lasting only a short period of time. They might then spend many months pushing lots of foliage. Species roses, for example, bloom only once in the spring, then spend four or five months scrambling around the garden sprouting new stems and leaves. Other plants bloom over a long period of time. Rose of Sharon is a slow grower that offers hibiscus-type flowers from early summer into fall, extending its branches while it grows.

Some plants, of course, are grown mostly for their foliage. These are the "evergreens" that stay green all year. They may offer some type of flower or fruit, but for the most part, this is not their main appeal. Hollies are wonderful evergreens, and have the bonus of a crop of red berries in winter. Junipers may be attractive but unremarkable in spring and summer, but when most deciduous plants have gone into deep dormancy, their green foliage and texture provide interest in an otherwise bare landscape.

All in all, select your plants for year-round appeal. Even if they lose foliage in the winter, deciduous plants can still provide unusual attraction. The bare branches of a Bradford pear against the winter skyline are quite handsome. Daphne offers wonderful late-winter fragrance.

MAINTENANCE

A key consideration in choosing a plant for your landscape is how much maintenance it will require. There are quite a few "lazy man's plants" that are perfect for the gardener who cares little for pruning, feeding or cultivating. Pittosporums require almost no care at all, especially if they are planted on the corners of the foundation. Other plants, some of which are quite easy to raise, require only minimal care, such as pruning a few times or spraying once a season for pests. But if you like a challenge, you'll find lots of opportunities. Hybrid roses will keep you busy as will daphne. Sargent crabapple is difficult to grow and gardenias need regular attention. The important thing about maintenance is to know how much is required and how much you are prepared to do before you purchase the plant.

GROWTH HABIT

In horticulture, the eventual size of a plant, its shape and how much time it takes to reach maturity is called "growth habit." You'll have to plan for this growth. Most plants will exceed their initial size simply because they will "grow up," and it's important to know how much they will grow. Nurserymen have a definite set of guidelines they use to determine how big a plant will get in size, and they classify plants accordingly. Plants from "low border" material to "shade trees" are usually displayed on the lot with "tell-tags" which describe their growth habit. Make sure your plant is the right size for the fit. All too often, homeowners have to remove plants because they grew too much or too little. In some cases, they will have to remove plants because they were planted too close to the house or sidewalk, or were mixed up with other plants and became hidden. Find out how much your plant will grow and how much time it will take to reach a mature size before you purchase it, because all the pruning you can do, and all the fertilizer in the warehouse won't make a plant perform in a size that doesn't fit.

OVERALL APPEAL

It goes without saying that you should plant only those shrubs which you will enjoy seeing as they develop over the years. Though there are no "ugly" plants in creation, there is no point including plants in your garden that you don't appreciate. Beyond that, "overall appeal" is the main consideration. A dynamic bloom habit might be coupled with other good features for a specimen that will provide years of enjoyment. Gardenias, for example, bring wonderful flowers and fragrance to your garden, and will also form excellent hedges or fine single, evergreen specimen plantings.

Other plants may be boring for eleven months, but once a year they'll offer superb flowers you don't mind waiting for. Slender deutzia is an excellent example of a landscape plant that graces the garden briefly but adds little for the rest of the year. Spider lilies are quite spectacular for a few weeks, but then fade quickly and disappear for another year.

Whether you choose a plant that flowers or fruits for many months (like pomegranates), or whether you select a landscape plant that never has an obvious flower (like Japanese holly), most of the ornamental shrubs available to you will provide some aesthetic quality. From the earliest days of spring, when witch hazel first shows a flower to the last days of winter when the bright green boughs of Leyland cypress come alive in the landscape, your choices for seasonal aesthetic appeal are abundant.

Finally, it does no good to plant a prime selection in a hidden location. If you like it, put it where you can see it and appreciate it. A nice plant tucked away in an obscure corner will soon be forgotten.

CHAPTER TWO

The Three Essentials: Sunlight, Water and Soil

SUNLIGHT

Nearly all plants, and certainly those that grow in open gardens, require sunlight. Sunlight is the fuel which feeds the very complicated and sophisticated engine of plant growth and development. For the most part, this is called photosynthesis—the process by which the plant converts sunlight to energy.

Plants require varying amounts of sunlight. Some will grow very well with just a little sunlight, and others will stand in the open sunshine, never drooping an inch on the hottest summer day. There is no standard, generally-applied rule about sunlight because the genetic makeup of each plant is different. But botanists know that sunshine is the blossom-maker. Without sufficient light many plants will simply not bloom. Plants grown in too deep shade tend to become "stretched" with elongated, thin stems and weak branches.

In our area, "full sun" means at least four hours of unshaded sunshine between eleven o'clock in the morning and four o'clock in the afternoon. For plants that require full sun (like verbena) a good place to put them is in the southeast garden. "Partial sun" is less than four hours of sunshine during the same period of time. Azaleas do very well in partial sun and are good choices for the southern garden. The darkest exposure is northern light, which is good for low-light growers like hydrangeas and English ivy which do not depend on sunshine to generate a flower. Hostas will bloom in a shade garden as will osmanthus. It is vital to know how much sunlight your plant needs to perform at peak levels.

One thing is generally accepted by most horticulturists. If you provide "dappled" light, which is filtered light as through a canopy of leaves, you'll probably grow better ornamentals. Few of our coastal landscape plants can take the direct summer sun because it generates too much heat. The fact that the plant wilts because of the heat is far more important than the amount of direct sunlight it receives. In many cases, the sunshine is so hot that it causes a plant to transpire more moisture than it can absorb through its roots.

WATER

Water is the life-support system of any plant. We all know this to be true from our own experiences with plants that wilt. The intricate vascular system of an ornamental plant uses water as a vehicle to move food up and down the stems. Water is also a key ingredient in photosynthesis. Besides moving vital molecules through the plant's tissues, water serves as the plant's air-conditioning system, the key to good root growth and the main ingredient in flower bud set. Azaleas, for example, will not set flower buds if they are subjected to long periods of drought in the spring, and dogwoods that lack sufficient water during the summer usually have inferior blossoms in the following year.

Roots grow where there is water. Many of our coastal plants, like azaleas and lawn grasses, have shallow root systems. This means they must seek moisture in the top six to ten inches of soil. It is vital to keep the water level high enough — and for long enough periods of time — for these shallow-growers to get all the moisture they need for a day's activity. And they need quite a bit! Many plants, especially vegetables, will move several gallons of water through their vascular systems in a single day.

If it is true that roots seek water, then it is also true that you should put the water where you want the roots to be. Steady, consistent watering is always better than drenching the soil around the plant whenever you see that it needs it. The general rule is to provide enough water to equal a half-inch every three days, or one inch per week for most plants in your landscape, including the grass in your lawn. You may need to provide more in hot, dry weather, or less when rainfall is adequate. Here, along the coast of the Carolinas, rainfall is often adequate. Your role as a caretaker is simply to supplement by applying deep drinks when your plant needs it the most.

Wilting foliage is a often a good indicator that your plant needs water, but not always. Some plants simply can't keep pace with the water available to them because they transpire moisture at a very rapid rate. They lose moisture much faster than the roots can absorb it. If your flower bed is well-watered but you notice excessive wilting, the solution may not be more water, but relocation to a shadier spot.

Keep in mind that too much water is as bad as too little. Plants move as much air up and down the stems as they do water. If you allow your plant to stand in "wet feet" it may drown — unable to absorb air through a waterlogged root system.

The best way to judge the correct amount is to measure the volume of water you use, not the amount of time you use it. A half-hour of watering may yield only a quarter-inch of water, but it could easily be more. You can test this with a simple tuna can. Place the empty can at the farthest point in the watering zone (either for an automatic irrigation system or for manual watering) and apply water until the can fills up. You will then have applied the correct amount. You may be surprised to find that it doesn't take as long to water the garden as you expected.

Soil

Obviously, sunlight and water work together to produce a healthy plant. But they are incomplete essentials without the third leg of the triangle — the soil in which the plant grows. Over the centuries, our soil has evolved into an amazing mass of nutrients, all of which are used to support life. Besides nitrogen, phosphorus and potassium, you'll find hundreds of other nutrients which feed a plant and play a vital role in photosynthesis. These nutrients are dissolved by the water, and are transported through the different parts of the plant. The ideal garden soil is super-rich in all nutrients, and is what horticulturists call "garden humus." Humus is a friable, textured blend of clay, sand and decaying matter. Though it is certainly possible to grow a plant in an "unbalanced" soil (one with too much clay or too much sand), it is always best to amend the soil of your garden so that it becomes ideal humus, which is the best soil possible.

One of the best ways to amend garden soil is to add large amounts of "compost." Compost, a mixture of decayed organic matter, neutralizes soil pH, adds extra nutrients to ordinary soil, and conditions the soil so that it is as close to an ideal medium as possible. Whether you scatter compost directly over an existing lawn, or mix it into a hole into which you are planting, it can be used at will. Vegetable growers measure amounts of compost in cubic yards, while an average gardener may use compost as a simple mulch, applied around the base of plants at the soil line.

Compost is easy to make. You can create a compost heap by adding vegetable kitchen scraps, lawn clippings, small prunings or just about any organic vegetation (except weeds) to a small confined pile of garden soil (about four or five square feet) and allowing it to decompose. By adding moderate amounts of water and by turning the mixture in the pile once a month or so, you'll soon create a "working" pile. Within several months you will generate the "black gold" that is so desirable as a growing medium.

Sunlight, water and soil. Good horticulture is a balance among these three essentials — whether balanced by nature or by the gardener. Without any one of them, your plant will not thrive.

CHAPTER THREE

The Plant in the Landscape

CONSIDER YOUR TERRAIN

Considering the type of terrain you have is an essential part of planning. Installing new plants in a flat place presents little challenge. Spacing is simple and the actual work can be done quickly. But digging holes and placing new plants on an uneven terrain is hard work. Judging the distance between plants, the angle at which they will grow and applying mulch takes time and thoughtful effort. Some plants will grow tall and erect regardless of the terrain, but many selections are ideal for slope coverage, like trailing junipers and miniature gardenias.

Water run-off is another vital consideration. Soil that washes away from flower beds will have to be replaced, but plants that adhere to slopes can control erosion and enhance the natural beauty of a sloping hillside. Keep in mind that you will have to cultivate the plants as you mow around them, weed the garden area, change the mulch and prune — and choose your plants accordingly .

MIXED BEDS

Throughout the planting guide, you'll see that the listed selections can be used in many ways. One of the favorites is as part of a mixed bed of ornamentals, especially when space is limited. With the taller plants positioned in the center or rear of the bed and shorter plants up front, the effect can be very pleasing. Mixed beds are usually combinations of plants that require little maintenance, or of plants with common cultural requirements. For example, azaleas mix well with camellias. Gardenias go well with osmanthus. You can mix a bed of ornamentals any way you choose, even taking advantage of shade trees and small flowering trees as anchors for your bed of shrubbery.

SPECIMEN PLANTS

A specimen plant is one placed all alone in the garden or yard to grow at will — showing off its individual good looks. Sasanquas make wonderful specimen plants as do well-established azaleas and small fruit trees. Prized ornamentals like one-of-a-kind hybrids, heirloom keepsakes and selected favorite plants can be placed by themselves in the garden. Specimen plants are easy to maintain because the area around the plant is usually free from other obstructions, allowing you to move around the plant at ease performing whatever task is needed to maintain it. Place a specimen where it can be seen from many angles, close to windows where it can easily be seen from the house or out in the open yard where it can be featured as a proud example.

MASSED PLANTINGS

Pure stands of specific varieties are often used in landscaping either as massed beds or as hedges. Ground-covering junipers are often planted in masses to cover a bank. Collections of hostas fill shaded nooks while clumps of daylilies offer a stunning display in sun. Plant groups of the same species where you want to see similar plant growth habits, and maintenance will be the same for the entire bed.

NATURAL AREAS

Natural areas are often incorporated into lawn sections of gardens when a homeowner chooses to allow the natural vegetation to grow at will, supplemented with a few cultivated varieties.

GARDENING WITH NATIVE PLANTS

A native plant is any plant that would have been found growing in the southeast coastal area prior to the arrival of the first Europeans. The wax myrtles the colonists saw thriving here are the same plants we recognize today. Virginia sweetspire was abundant then as it is now. Today's popular pines were the dominant trees of the of the fourteenth century, and yaupons grew along the coast and in the pine barrens of colonial Carolina. Some of our popular vines and climbers like trumpet vine and jessamine were abundant years ago as was American holly. Leucothoe was also popular among the colonists. Some of these "natives" were "adapted" by either cross-breeding, or simply by bringing them into cultivation. Azaleas were adapted quite easily, as were many perennials like mist flower, coreopsis, and spiderwort.

In today's modern landscapes homeowners tend to plant whatever their local nurseries decide to offer. There's not a lot of difference between gardens of southern Texas, northern Virginia or coastal Carolina, simply because people tend to use the plants that are regionally popular. But what can make your garden here in coastal Carolina unique is not only the environment in which you are working, but also the plants you choose to grow. By using some selected native plants in your landscape plan, you'll identify your garden as a special place.

There is a practical reason to use natives as well. Because they have survived here for centuries, chances are good they'll perform well in your garden, free from pests or the management problems presented by new varieties.

Simply because a plant grows well in natural surroundings doesn't mean it will grow well in cultivation. A plant that thrives along a sandy ridge in the country may not perform in your well-tended garden. The botanical make-up of the plant may not allow it to. Plants grow in certain conditions because they are ideally suited for them. When placed in altered surroundings, like well-fertilized lawns or irrigated group plantings, they may not perform at all. It's important to duplicate a native plant's environment as closely as possible, but it's important to realize that some native plants may not grow in your home landscape. Your nurseryman can help you make the decision. If you decide to include a few natives in your garden you should make sure you purchase them from a lawn and garden center or nursery rather than digging them from the wild. Many species are protected, and harvesting them from the wild is against the law. In any case, you will lose valuable roots when you take a plant from its native site. This can cause years of delay while the plant repairs the damage done by digging it, plus many months of recuperation as the plant adapts to new surroundings.

SOME SPECIFIC NATIVE PLANT SUGGESTIONS

There are quite a few native plants readily available in nurseries and garden centers, but here are a few favorites that will grace your garden and offer supreme local appeal:

American holly
bald cypress
Carolina bay
common magnolia
coreopsis
Eastern red cedar
fennel
leucothoe
maples
mist flower
pines
sweet gum
trumpet vine
tupelo
Virginia sweetspire
wax myrtle
yaupon
yucca

CHAPTER FOUR

The Mechanics of Plant Installation

PLANT SOURCES

Where you purchase your plant and how much you pay for it are not as important as making sure you have the healthiest stock possible. Of course, as with all major purchases, it helps to deal with an established vendor. Most modern nurserymen are trained to offer excellent stock and competent advice. But regardless of your source, take time to choose obviously healthy, top grade material. Two-for-one deals on inferior plants may cause you to spend years cultivating unsightly material, whereas full price purchases may provide immediate attraction without the need for spending time repairing your plants.

Nursery stock is offered for sale in a number of different ways. Plants that have been raised in pots are known as "container grown." This is perhaps the best method of purchasing, because transplant shock from the pot to your garden is significantly reduced. Field-produced plants are often referred to as "line out stock" or "liners." The nursery will dig these plants for you as you select them from the rows. "B&B" plants are balled and burlapped. The root systems are covered with burlap. These plants should be installed intact, allowing the burlap to decay naturally as the plant grows. Some newer methods of selling stock include biodegradable cardboard boxes and paper bags, both of which are good methods, but the packaging can be awkward to handle and the root systems can be hindered from good future development because of their confinement in early stages. The least acceptable is "bare root" stock that contains no soil. Try to avoid bare roots whenever possible, as the chances of survival are reduced.

Regardless of the way you purchase your plant, how you take it home may have the most influence on its future survival. Protection from winds and hot sun are essential, so make sure your new purchase is well-shielded. Don't allow the wind to rake it, and when you get it home, water it well and store it in a cool, protected place until you are ready to plant it.

INSTALLING YOUR NEW PLANT

Dig the hole twice as large as the existing root ball and place your plant in it, so that the mound of roots forms a slight convex curve at the surface. If the new plant creates a concave curve in the hole, you've planted too deeply, which is the largest cause of new plant failure. Back-fill the hole with fresh soil making sure you eliminate all air pockets by tamping the soil firmly. Build a small earthen dam around the plant and give it an inch of water every day for a week. It's just this simple. Don't prune it, don't add any fertilizer to the hole, and don't disturb it. There'll be plenty of time for all these things later as you begin to cultivate your new plant several months after you plant it.

CHAPTER FIVE

Weeds and Insects

There are three pests you'll face in the garden — weeds, insects and disease. In some cases, you'll encounter cultural problems that don't relate to these three, like improper pruning or running over a plant as you back down the driveway. And in a few remote cases, you'll have some environmental problems like lightning strikes or hurricanes. But for the most part, the three major pests will give you the most challenge as you cultivate your garden plants. In this chapter we address weeds and insects.

WEEDS

A weed is any plant growing where you don't want it to grow, and these plants should be eliminated. Weeds harbor insects and diseases. They also extract moisture and vital nutrients from the soil and crowd plants in the garden, preventing them from gaining the space they need to expand. It is very important to keep weeds out of the ornamental flower bed, and the most effective way of keeping the weeds out is simply by pulling them by hand, or repeatedly cutting them down.

THE REPEATED CUTTING METHOD OF WEED CONTROL

Even the most invasive weeds cannot tolerate repeated cutting. A leaf is the one part the plant needs to manufacture energy, and when it is denied the ability to produce foliage it can't survive. Since most weeds are annuals, repeated cutting will prevent future generations because the plant will not be allowed to flower. The one-two punch of cutting the foliage and cutting the flowers will destroy the plant because it will not be able to produce energy for itself, nor will it be able to reproduce.

Repeated cutting is time-consuming, and you'll have to assign it as a weekly garden task, but if you approach it as you would any other garden chore, you will eventually gain control of most weed problems. You can use any garden tool in the arsenal for repeated cutting, whether it be a line trimmer or shears. If you approach your weeding tools the same way you would approach a herbicide, you'll be able to use them wisely, avoiding sensitive plants, and attacking only those you wish to eliminate.

WEED BLOCKS

Professional landscapers have used organic weed blocks for many years to control weeds in ornamental flower beds, around shrubbery and in vegetable gardens. These weed blocks include sheets of black plastic which are spread over the garden soil before it is planted, landscape fabric which is used the same way, and heavy organic mulch. Black plastic is very effective, but it does not allow water and nutrients to pass into the soil beneath it. Landscape fabric is an improvement over plastic, but may allow some weeds to pop up over time. Garden mulch is excellent because it prevents most weeds from invading the flower bed and helps to protect the plants' root systems as well. Of course, the main advantage of garden mulch is that it can be replaced at will, and is completely organic. Mulch actually helps many plants by providing a source of some nutrients.

HERBICIDES

It's always easier to weed a little every day than it is to face a healthy stand of weeds twice a year. But sometimes, a pair of gloves, a face mask and an hour or two of labor are too much, even on a cool day. You might choose one of the hundreds of commercial herbicides on the market to help you.

There are a great many herbicides, many of which can be used by the home gardener quite simply and safely, if the label instructions are followed carefully. It's important to know your target and to choose the type of weed killer that best suits the purpose.

• *Post-Emergent vs. Pre-Emergent* Herbicides destroy plant life in many ways. Some kill foliage out-right. Others interfere with a plant's ability to reproduce. Post-emergent weed killers destroy plants after they emerge from the ground. Pre-emergent herbicides prevent a plant from germinating. The pre-emergents are very effective in killing weeds in lawn grasses before they become invasive. Atrazine and Purge are examples of pre-emergent herbicides. When used correctly and at the right time of year, pre-emergent herbicides are very effective in eliminating weeds from lawn grasses before they become active plants in the lawn.

• *Nonspecific Herbicides* Some weed killers kill the foliage of any plant. In many cases they will also kill the roots. These "nonspecific weed killers" use strong chemicals to destroy plant tissues, and should be used only when all other weeding techniques have failed. Often sold in pre-mixed liquid form, bottles of these herbicides may have sprayers attached for easy dispensing. Another type is a granular product that destroys plant life in any area where the material is scattered.

Next to fertilizers, pre-mixed liquid herbicides are the most popular items sold in most lawn and garden centers, and are used by many homeowners to control everything from dandelion plants to difficult weeds like pennywort. It is important to use these weed killers carefully, making sure that you spray only the foliage you intend to kill, avoiding drifting spray and following the instructions on the label to the letter.

•*Specific herbicides*
Some weed killers destroy only specific plants or their foliage, leaving others completely unaffected. Usually sold in granular form or concentrated liquids, these herbicides are used around ornamental flower beds, killing invasive weeds over a long period of time. The label will indicate targeted weeds and which plants' root zones are not affected by it. You'll have to be very careful if you decide to use a specific herbicide because, in many cases, it will harm a few plants you wish to keep. A perennial flower bed mixed with some ornamental shrubs is a prime danger zone for damage by specific herbicides, because even though the chemical make-up of these herbicides is fairly exact, there may

be some plants you wish to maintain as perennials that the herbicide classifies as weeds. If you use a specific herbicide, make sure you read the label carefully and that you know your target.

Before you use a commercial herbicide, consider all the alternatives. Simple weekly weeding, done as a garden chore, is probably the best method of controlling weeds. If you use a sensible combination of garden mulch, regular weeding by hand and repeated cutting of exposed weeds, you'll probably never have a problem with the garden's number one pest. And there is every chance that you will be able to avoid herbicides as well.

INSECTS

Insects are usually not the problem many gardeners believe them to be. Of course, they can get out of hand if they are allowed to roam in large numbers. For the sake of simplicity, we'll group all the culprits of the garden we think are insects under that heading, though some creatures are technically not insects. For example, caterpillars, some bugs and worms are not insects. But, in any event, we will label the "bad guys" insects for purposes of this discussion.

The choices for killing insects are many, from pre-mixed sprays to highly concentrated powders that require mixing. Unfortunately, most gardeners prefer the simplicity of broad-based insecticides that kill a large variety of garden creatures indiscriminately. However, before you use an insecticide, consider the following points:

•*Not all creatures are bad*. Many insects perform valuable tasks in the garden, even destroying other harmful insects. Ladybeetles destroy aphids. Some flies feed on dangerous insects. Earthworms perform valuable tasks in the soil by breaking down organic matter, fertilizing the garden with their "castings" and helping to aerate the ground. Honey bees are essential for pollination, and caterpillars transform into the butterflies we find so appealing in the landscape. A broad-based insecticide may kill all these beneficial insects as well as the culprits.

•*You may not need an insecticide at all*. Most professional horticulturists consider as much as twenty percent foliage loss to insects to be acceptable.

•*Often, the most effective insecticide is a steady stream of forced water*. A strong stream of water can clean aphids from plant stems, eliminate mealybugs, knock out spider webs and eliminate caterpillars from ornamental shrubs.

•*Nature has an excellent way of taking care of itself*. Birds feed on many insects, a stiff winter can destroy large numbers of harmful creatures before they emerge in the spring, and plants have many ways of resisting attacks from most insects. It is entirely possible that you may not have to do anything at all in the face of an insect problem, but let nature handle the problem itself.

•*Use some of the things you have close at hand before you use a commercial insecticide.* A hand-held vacuum is effective against clouds of whitefly. Soapy water is a basic cleaner that gets rid of caterpillars. And an alcohol swab will solve scale problems.

• *A few flea beetles, a worm or two, or even a group of hungry bugs can be simply swept into a bag and destroyed without harming you, the host plant or the environment.*

But, after all, if you need an insecticide use one that is safe and effective. It is always best to use a specific insecticide that targets the problem insect directly, leaving others alone.

ORGANICS-THE FIRST LINE OF DEFENSE

In today's landscape, concern for the environment should be the first consideration. Using insecticides wisely fits that idea, and perhaps the "cleanest" insecticides are organic in nature. Many organic insect killers are actually naturally-occurring chemicals or materials that have been refined, enhanced and packaged for use by consumers in home gardens. Though not always labeled as organic, they should be easy to find in the lawn and garden center, especially if you get some help from the folks at the sales counter. Many are branded products. But don't let that confuse you. Most organic bug killers are derived from natural things you can quickly identify if you read the label carefully. In this book, you will find the following organic insecticides mentioned frequently as the first line of defense against bugs that are affecting your prized ornamentals.

• *Pyrethrins:* Derived from poisonous flowers, these broad-based insect killers stun and destroy many insects.

• *Rotenone:* This poison is deadly against cold-blooded creatures, but has no effect on warm-blooded animals. Made from the roots of poisonous plants, it is often combined with pyrethrins for a more effective punch.

• *Bt: Bacillus thuringiensis* is a bacteria that targets many pests, from mosquito larvae to caterpillars, but is especially deadly to worms because it destroys their ability to eat. Bt is very safe in the environment and can be used as often as needed as long as you follow the label instructions carefully.

• *DE: Diotomaceous earth* is a material made by grinding the fossilized remains of ancient marine life called diotoms. The results are tiny, razor-sharp particles that are used to control fleas, ticks and soft-bodied insects like snails and slugs which cannot move across bands of DE without cutting themselves to shreds. Though deadly to soft-bodied creatures, it has no effect on warm-blooded animals. DE is sold in several forms, one of which is used in swimming pool filters. Be sure to purchase horticultural grade DE, a more highly refined product for use in the home garden.

SYNTHETIC INSECTICIDES

The chemical shelf of the lawn and garden center will contain many synthetic bug killers. These are insecticides produced by chemical companies for use in home gardens, and may contain some naturally occurring ingredients in combination with laboratory-produced materials. There are many from which to choose, including some old standbys that have been used for many years. Synthetics offer some advantages over organics, especially in the speed with which they kill culprits. Some synthetics are less expensive than organics, and they often have more applications, killing a wider range of insects.

Whether you choose an organic or a synthetic insecticide, follow some basic rules:

Know your target and make sure you want to kill it.
Protect yourself, regardless of the type of insecticide, by wearing protective clothing, gloves and a mask.
Read the label instructions carefully and follow them to the letter. Using more than you need may cause problems in the garden, and using less than the recommended amount may result in repeated applications which can be just as harmful.

Garden insecticides are abundant. But as you can see, they also pose choices for responsible gardeners. If you choose wisely you can enjoy a safe garden that is dominated by beneficial insects and is a welcoming place for those of us who appreciate a garden's natural beauty.

CHAPTER SIX

Plant Diseases

Even the most experienced horticulturist will find the diagnosis of plant diseases very difficult. This is probably because so many cultural problems in the garden cause conditions that resemble pathogenic situations. A cluster of yellowing, sickly leaves can be caused by a soil pH imbalance, by too much water, by disturbed roots, by animal markings, by fertilizer "burns" or by fungal infection. It may take a plant pathologist to determine the cause and solution. But here along the southeast coast you can be assured that the heat and humidity will eventually create the perfect environment for some, if not many, plant diseases.

FUNGI

A fungus is actually a plant. But it usually lacks a typical vascular system and plant parts that synthesize sunlight. Athlete's foot is a typical fungus. So is the mold that grows on stale bread, the "soot" that covers shoes in a damp, dark summer closet, or the toadstools and mushrooms that appear in your lawn. Not all fungi are bad. Some work deep in the soil of the garden, breaking down organic matter to help create organisms that benefit plant growth and development. Mushrooms are good examples of helpful fungi. But some fungi are dangerous, poisoning plants and the animals that handle them.

Fungi spread through the garden in a number of ways. They hitch rides on anything that moves across the landscape, they spread on water droplets, cruise through the air on breezes or contaminate clean surfaces by rubbing against them. Once established they cause damage by feeding on fresh plant material, using the plant's healthy tissue as a source for their own nutrition.

PREVENTION IS THE BEST TREATMENT

Eliminating the breeding ground is the best treatment for most dangerous fungi. You'd be surprised at the number of fungal disorders you can eliminate by keeping the garden clean, weed-free and dry. Just simple garden sanitation is the key to keeping flower beds healthy and disease-free. Here are some recommendations from the professionals on how to accomplish that:

- *Don't over-water.* Too much water around plants can set up the perfect conditions for fungal growth.
- *Weeds harbor all sorts of pests, including fungi.* Keep the weeds down, and you'll keep fungi at bay.
- *Don't let spent flowers accumulate on the ground.* Rake flowers after they fall, and keep the area around plants clean.
- *Water early in the morning so the sun will help evaporate the moisture that carries plant disease.*
- *Keep your tools clean.*
- *Don't work around plants that are wet.*

• *Provide plenty of sunlight and air circulation.*Crowded plants attract fungal disease, so keep your ornamental beds open and dry.
• *Prune away infected parts of plants so that they will not infect healthy tissue.*

There are thousands of fungi and hundreds of commercial fungicides, both organic and synthetic. At some point, you will probably need a fungicide to help you control disease and maintain a healthy garden. Fungicides work in a number of ways to restore health, but for the most part, they set up barriers which prevent the spread of disease. That is why it is so important to treat the entire garden area or the entire plant in question, because once plant tissue has been infected by a fungus, it rarely responds to a fungicide. You'll need to help healthy tissue resist the fungus as it attempts to spread.

BAKING SODA — THE ANCIENT CURE

As if the thousands of uses for which baking soda is famous were not enough, here is yet another excellent use — as a garden fungicide. Simply mix a quarter cup of baking soda in a gallon of water and spray it over the leaves and stems of the plant and around the base near the soil line. Common mildew, mold and some petal blights are prevented from spreading by this simple mixture. Apply this fungicide every ten days until you gain control.

COMMERCIAL FUNGICIDES

We often mention commercial fungicides in the descriptive section of the book because serious plant problems may require these fast-acting and convenient forms of fungal control. Commercial fungicides are mentioned as treatments for serious fungal disorders like brown patch in lawns, septoria leaf spot in dogwoods, or petal blight in azaleas. You can usually get some excellent advice on fungicides from the sales folks at the lawn and garden center. Or you can take a sample of the problem to your local plant clinic at a Cooperative Extension Service office. In either case, chances are good that you'll find a fungicide readily available to treat your problems. Remember to follow the rules by reading the label carefully, following instructions to the letter and wearing protective clothing. Keep in mind that any disease treatment will alter the environment in which a plant grows. Using a fungicide can be very helpful for sick plants, but can cause problems in healthy plants if it is applied incorrectly.

WHEN IN DOUBT

It is hard to diagnose plant diseases, much less determine the correct treatment. If you have doubts about a plant's condition, ask some simple questions first, and seek some professional advice.

• *Is the disorder spreading to other plant parts or other areas of the garden?* If so, chances are good it is a disease, not a cultural problem.
• *Do you see swollen areas of plant tissue, soft or rotting material, oozing or open lesions?* These conditions

usually indicate disease.
• *Is there evidence of unusual growths, strangely-colored spots, dramatic puckering, leaf-rolling or foliage loss?* These are signs that a fungus is working on healthy tissue.

Whenever you are in doubt about conditions or treatments, professional help is close at hand. State universities in cooperation with local governments operate plant clinics in most extension offices. Here you may find labs and diagnostic services, and you will always find professionals that are quick to offer excellent advice. These facilities are usually listed in your telephone directory under "State Cooperative Extension Service."

VIRUSES, NEMATODES AND BACTERIA

Even more difficult to diagnose than fungi are these three complex organisms. Like everything else in nature, viruses, nematodes and bacteria can be good or bad. The viruses that cause stippling in the leaves of tomatoes can be very bad for good fruit production. But the virus that creates the variegation in the leaves of golden euonymous is essential to the plant's appearance. Nematodes can destroy the root system of an aucuba, but they can also destroy the insects which feed on the leaves of an aucuba plant. Bacteria can leave whole sections of lawn grass looking bleak, but they also work with other organisms deep in the soil to create rich garden humus that is so desirable for good plant growth.

For the average homeowner, these three things rarely cause major problems. And that's a lucky thing for gardeners because there isn't much that can be done when they become harmful garden pests. There are no available cures for most garden viruses, the chemical treatments for nematodes are expensive and often require professional assistance, and bacteriacides are usually ineffective. Because of the complex nature of diagnosis and treatment, it's always best to have a professional horticulturist help you with disease problems that you suspect are not fungal in nature. Try the Cooperative Extension Service as a starting point for professional advice.

Disease control is not simple. But remember that prevention is the best solution. Chances are good that you'll never have to treat a sick plant if you prevent sickness by keeping the plants healthy, weed-free and vigorous. But when all else fails, don't hesitate to solve your problems quickly and effectively. There's no point in spending time and money developing a quality landscape, only to have it ruined because of an unchecked disease. When you view your garden from any angle, you deserve to see vibrant, healthy plants, not only for your own enjoyment but for the overall healthy appeal it offers to your neighborhood

CHAPTER SEVEN

Pests That Are Almost As Big As You

LARGER ANIMALS

As development encroaches on the territory of native wildlife and as our rural communities become more urban, we are apt to see more wild animals in our gardens. Rabbits eat plants, squirrels dig in the garden, moles tunnel under lawns, and even deer browse through hedges. Dogs and cats become more obvious too, as our neighborhoods become more populated. Whether the critters that upset the garden are large or small, there is usually a deterrent that safely controls them or at least encourages them to move away. Here are some of the common tricks you can use in your own garden to manage the problems caused by larger animals.

• *Rabbits-* Scatter some black pepper over the leaves of target plants, or mix up a spray of two gallons of water to which you add a bottle of red pepper sauce, a bottle of Texas Pete, a teaspoon of dish detergent and a tablespoon of household ammonia. Sprayed around areas that are affected by larger animals, this mixture will usually irritate them enough to make them leave.

•*Squirrels-* Cover your bulbs and new seeds with a layer of chicken wire before you apply your garden mulch. This will prevent squirrels from digging in sensitive places. Or you can use the pepper trick we mentioned in the section on rabbits.

• *Moles-* These are not usually a problem unless they cause you to trip in the soft soil of their tunnels. They heave the soil, which makes the lawn unsightly, but rarely causes damage to the roots of the plants. By themselves, moles do not create harmful situations. But in some cases, field rats and voles (an animal similar to a mole but with an appetite for plant parts rather than worms and grubs) will follow the same tunnels. Interrupt the feeding habits of moles by using a lawn grass insecticide that destroys the mole's food supply.

• *Dogs and Cats-* Use one of the animal repellents like "Repel" or "Ropel" which are sold in most lawn and garden centers. The pepper spray, or ordinary black pepper scattered on the leaves of selected plants will also repel most dogs and cats.

• *Deer-* These are more serious pests. Barrier hedges of pyracantha or Spanish bayonet (Yucca) along the garden border, pepper sprays and chemical repellents usually work over a period of time, but be patient and diligent. It may take some persistence and time to gain control, but you will eventually cause more problems for hungry deer than they think it is worth.

THE BIGGEST PEST IN THE GARDEN

The one pest that causes the most damage among your plants and flowers is probably you! Over-treating with pesticides, over-watering, using too much fertilizer and damaging plants with garden tools create far more problems than the forces of nature. Pest control begins with self-control and common sense. If you think through your problems, know your target and follow the rules, you are probably on your way to a healthy garden. You will usually find that helping nature solve her problems is far easier than assuming the task on your own. And it will be far easier keeping the balance of health and vigor over problems and diseases, if you never have to correct the mistakes you have made in trying to control pests.

CHAPTER EIGHT

Fertilizers and Soil pH

WHAT MAKES UP A FERTILIZER?

All fertilizers have an "NPK" ratio. These three elements are essential for plant growth. These letters stand for nitrogen (N), phosphorus (P) and potassium or potash (K). Nitrogen is the element that greens a plant and promotes good leaf growth and green color. It stimulates top growth and new foliage. Phosphorus is the element that produces flowering potential and is the fruit-setter. Though usually available in our soils without boosting, supplemental doses are often recommended because some plants need extra amounts to perform at peak levels. Potash is the root builder, and helps a plant develop good health as well as a strong immune system. Potash promotes strong cell growth and aids in the transfer of nutrients through the vascular system.

By law, a bag, box or can of fertilizer must state what's in it, in the way of nitrogen, phosphorus and potash. The elements are always listed in that order. The numbers you see on the label are stated in percentages of these three elements. An NPK of 10-10-10 would be ten percent each of the elements nitrogen, phosphorus and potash. If the bag of fertilizer weighed one hundred pounds, ten pounds of it would be nitrogen, ten pounds would be phosphorus and ten pounds potash. The rest of the bag, seventy pounds, would be other ingredients.

If the NPK is 8-8-8 or 10-10-10, or the percentages are relatively close, the fertilizer is called "balanced." An example of a fertilizer that is not balanced is 0-0-24, the formula for a popular NPK called Sul-Po-Mag or K-Mag. This blend is rich in potash, but contains none of the other main ingredients.

Sometimes a fertilizer will contain other ingredients that might enhance a plant's development. Often, these other ingredients are called "micronutrients" or "trace elements." The trace elements include zinc, copper, molybdenum and iron, among other things.

A fertilizer that contains all these trace elements is called a "complete" fertilizer. An example of a complete fertilizer is Harvester Brand 6-6-12. Besides six percent nitrogen, six percent phosphorus and twelve percent potash, Harvester contains all the trace elements that may be lacking in other formulas. Unless it is otherwise recommended, you should aim for a complete, balanced formula.

In some cases, the recommendation will be something different, like 0-0-24 (Sul-Po-Mag), or 0-30-0, the NPK for superphosphate. These formulas are recommended because a plant at a given stage in development may require more of one nutrient and less of another.

WATER-SOLUBLE VS GRANULAR

The planting guides in this book usually recommend granular fertilizers. These are the formulas which are poured from a bag or box, applied to the soil around the base of the plant, and watered into the ground. The granules of fertilizer are broken down slowly by water and soil microbes until they become available to the plant's roots. These grains of fertilizer, in the form of various nutrients are then absorbed into the plant's system. Usually this process is the best way for a plant to gain extra nutrients.

Water-soluble plant foods are packaged concentrates of various plant nutrients. When mixed with water, these concentrates become readily available plant food containing all the elements listed on the label of the brand you choose. Like granular formulas, the water-soluble fertilizer will have an NPK ratio. There is a definite advantage to using water-soluble formulas, namely the immediate action of the fertilizer. Unlike granular formulas, water-solubles don't have to be broken down over time. They are quick acting. Some water-soluble fertilizers claim the additional benefit of "foliar feeding." This is the concept that water-soluble plant food can be absorbed by the leaves of the plant as well as the roots. Though this idea has been debated by horticulturists, there is some evidence that plants take nutrients through their leaves.

There are some drawbacks to using water-soluble plant foods. Though they are usually complete formulas, they rarely contain trace elements, and for most garden plants these micronutrients are vital to plant growth. Water-solubles dissipate rapidly, too. The sandy soils of the coastal area simply don't retain moisture long enough for the plant to absorb nutrients effectively unless they are "presented" to the root system over a long period of time, as they are with granulars. As a result, you'll have to use water-solubles on a regular basis, and you'll get better results if you use a "sticker-spreader" that helps the material cling to the roots a little longer. This is why many horticulturists advise adding a dash of dish detergent to the formulas you use, so that they will spread through the soil easily and stick to the object for a longer period of time.

Plants which are fed with regular water-soluble fertilizers usually show quick results, and often the results are remarkable. But water-soluble usage has to be repeated many times for the plant to maintain its appearance over a growing season. Unless you plan on using these formulas regularly, it's best not to start using them, but stay with a granular application.

The exception to this may be feeding hanging baskets and potted plants, which usually cannot tolerate granular formulas because of the concentrated nature of their growing media. But if you decide to use a water-soluble formula, for whatever purpose, it's always a good idea to "enhance" it by adding some organic ingredients. These additions will provide trace elements which can compliment your feeding program. Try this formula for containerized plants, hanging baskets and some selected garden plants, like perennials and annuals.Mix a full gallon of your favorite water-soluble formula, following the label instructions carefully. Add a tablespoon of kelp meal or liquid kelp, a tablespoon of fish emulsion, a tablespoon of Epsom salts, a teaspoon of dish detergent and a tablespoon of baking soda. Shake the container often while you pour so that you'll keep the mixture in suspension, and don't try to store it longer than five or six days. If you use kelp meal rather than liquid kelp, remember that it is not water-soluble, so you'll have to pour it rather than spray it through a sprayer. Here is what you'll be getting from these additions: Kelp is a seaweed extract which is extra-rich in phosphorous as well as many trace elements. Fish emulsion is an ancient source of nitrogen as well as countless other nutrients. Epsom salts will provide magnesium, an element often lacking in fertilizer formulas. The baking soda will act as a brief fungicide and will help reduce the odor of the formula, and the dish detergent is the agent which will cause the formula to stick and spread. You can use this formula for all your plants, and you can use it every two weeks, or simply follow the label instructions on the container of the water-soluble base formula you have chosen. One of the direct advantages of this formula, as with all water-solubles, is that you run very little risk of chemical plant burn due to overuse.

TIMED-RELEASE FORMULAS

Fertilizers sold as timed-release brands are becoming quite popular for gardeners because of their convenience and safety. These highly concentrated prills contain all the essential elements in various size capsules with various degrees of coatings. As they break down over a period of time, they release their nutrients into the soil. Timed-release formulas are easy to use, quite safe in the garden and provide a combination of water-soluble plant food and granular applications. Sold under a number of different labels, the timed-release formulas often take the form of gray, brown or white prills which are easily spotted on the soil surface of many container-grown plants. They are often the fertilizer of choice for nurserymen.

FERTILIZER SAFETY

Regardless of the formula you choose, it is essential that you follow the label carefully and that you not fall into the trap of thinking "more is better." Fertilizers contain many things which can upset the balance of the soil for many months if they are used in excess, and the result can be dangerous. The nonsynthetic granular formulas contain nitrogen which has a high salt content, and when used improperly these salts can cause a "burned" appearance. Using a premium grade, synthetic formula such as 16-4-8 allows you to avoid this problem.

Use fertilizers in the correct season. It's never a good idea to feed plants while they are dormant. It's always best to apply fertilizers when the plant can use them the best — just before blooming and just before they begin to grow.

PROTECTING THE ENVIRONMENT

Unless we curb the use of high nitrogen fertilizers, we will see a continuation of the negative effects on our waterways, ponds and lakes. As fertilizers wash from our sidewalks, driveways and parking lots, or as they get caught in run-off collection areas they create side effects which harm the environment and appearance of the area. The coastal area has current problems with algae blooms in nearly every pond, and our natural waterways — the prized feature of our land — are becoming the depository of excessive fertilizers. Though golf courses and large public lawns and gardens certainly contribute to the problem, homeowners and consumers are the biggest culprits. Do your share of helping keep our area clean and beautiful by using only the fertilizer you need and no more. It's crucial that you use low nitrogen formulas, and make sure you know your target. Spreading any amount of fertilizer on the driveway, street or parking area is wasteful and harmful.

FORMULAS AND FERTILIZERS YOU WILL FIND MENTIONED FREQUENTLY IN THIS GUIDE

8-8-8 is a well-balanced formula, sold in most lawn and garden centers. Look for a "premium" brand that offers trace elements.

10-10-10 is the same as 8-8-8, but slightly more powerful and usually more economical because you'll apply less of it than a lower NPK.

5-10-10 is an excellent formula to use when slightly lower nitrogen is satisfactory. This popular blend is often the formula you'll find recommended in the guide.

6-6-12 Originally made for vegetable growers, this specialty formula is rich in trace elements and will give excellent results in the flower garden as well as mixed ornamental beds.

5-10-30 The formula used for starting some lawns in the spring, this low nitrogen fertilizer is heavy in potash so that it builds roots before it promotes top growth.

5-0-15 Centipede Plus Brand with Iron is one of the few branded products mentioned in the guide. Specifically for centipedegrass lawns, this formula releases nitrogen over a three-month period, so it is environmentally friendly and time-saving because it is used only once or twice during the growing season.

14-4-14 is used to jump start lawns and gardens when heavy rains or other conditions have left the landscape depleted of nutrients.

16-4-8 Another slow-release formula, this timed fertilizer is used for the heavy feeders, Saint Augustine grass, Bermuda grass and Zoysia grass. Look for a Royster-Clark label.

Sul-Po-Mag or **K-Mag** is mentioned frequently in the guide, and is used to stimulate a plant's bloom potential and root system. It has an NPK of 0-0-24, but is rich in several other plant nutrients. This formula can be used well ahead of blooming, even in late dormancy.

Superphosphate 0-30-0 is the NPK for this source of phosphorus. Derived from rock phosphate, it is slow to break down in the soil but provides a wonderful source of bloom-making material.

Bonemeal Like superphosphate, this source of phosphorus is derived from ground bones and usually has an NPK of 0-10-0.

Greensand The result of mining operations in New Jersey, this material comes from the floor of the Atlantic. Containing countless trace elements, it is super-rich in potash and has been used for many years as a plant developer. Greensand is a staple in the organic gardener's cabinet.

A homemade specialty blend from "Dr. Plant" You can create your own individual formula by mixing the following ingredients: 1 part bloodmeal (a source of slow-release organic nitrogen derived from animal processing), 2 parts superphosphate and 2 parts Sul-Po-Mag. The formula will be low in nitrogen, but higher in phosphorus and potash and will contain many trace elements. Use it carefully at the same rate you would 5-10-10.

SOIL PH

The expression "pH" is from the French phrase 'pouvoir hydrogene' which translates roughly as "hydrogen power." Though chemists use this term frequently for various purposes, it directly relates to the acidity or alkalinity of any material, and for home gardeners, the material is garden soil.

Soils east of the Mississippi are usually acid in nature, not alkaline. There are some exceptions but, for the most part, you'll be dealing with soil that is slightly acid in nature. The pH scale is broad — from one to fourteen, seven being neutral. The higher the scale number, the more alkaline the soil. The lower the scale number, the more acidic the soil. Soils which have a pH of four or five are considered acidic. Below that, they are probably too acidic and will need to be adjusted. Many of the landscape plants mentioned in the book grow best in neutral pH, though some will grow very well in slightly acid soil.

TESTING THE SOIL'S PH

Once a year, you should have a complete soil analysis done by the Cooperative Extension Service to determine the exact makeup of your garden soil. The test, usually provided at a small handling charge, will give you all sorts of vital information about your soil, especially the pH. The Extension office can give you the details of how to sample your soil, and they will usually provide the containers for sampling. It's best to test the soil in the spring when the garden warms, but it may take several months to adjust the pH, so fall-testing is often recommended.

The test results provided by the Extension Service are detailed. But if all you want to determine is the acidity of a particular soil sample, you can do it quickly yourself, any time you choose. Lawn and garden centers offer a number of test kits for home use. They range from expensive meters to simple, one-time litmus tests. Some soil testers can be used more than once, others are quick-read, disposable meters. Use the tester that fits the purpose, and as soon as you are sure of the relative acidity of the soil, amend it accordingly so you'll adjust the soil to a more suitable pH.

Keep in mind that many horticulturists claim soil pH as the most crucial element in raising healthy plants. If the soil is too acidic, many major nutrients become "locked-up" and will be useless to the plant. The difference between a healthy, vibrant landscape and one that always looks tired and weak could simply be a bag or two of limestone, not fertilizers or pesticides. Nearly every one of the plant guides in this book recommends pH testing at least once a year, and appropriate follow-up with soil amendments.

Changing the soil pH is not a complicated process if you follow one of the basic plans and schedules listed below:

•*Limestone*   There are two types of limestone available, calcitic and dolomitic. Though both come from minerals that are mined in quarries, dolomitic is probably the best type because it contains both magnesium and calcium which are released slowly into the soil. Limestone increases the pH of the soil by reducing acidity and encouraging bacterial activity. The label will direct you on proper usage, but a general rule is to apply five pounds of limestone per hundred square feet of garden area to raise the pH by one point. A two-pound coffee can will hold about six pounds of limestone.

•*Wood ashes*   When spread over your garden area, wood ashes may be the fastest and strongest soil amendment you can use. Besides containing a high percentage of calcium carbonate, the material which actually does the the reducing of acid, wood ashes contain many valuable trace elements like boron, zinc and sulfur, as well as significant amounts of phosphorus and potassium. One of the disadvantages of using wood ashes is that you have to have a ready source, and it takes quite a bit to adjust the pH. When mixed with water, ashes produce lye, which can burn plant tissue. Use wood ashes as a short term, quick fix only. It's best to mix them with some other ingredient as a carrier — like sharp sand (the yellow sand found on construction lots, also called "builder's sand") — which will make it easier to spread. It is not a good idea to simply spread ashes over the garden or around plants. Use forty pounds of hardwood ashes over a thousand square feet to adjust the pH up by one point. A two-pound coffee can holds about two pounds of sifted ashes.

•*Compost* is nature's best way to adjust soil pH. It takes awhile to do it, but you can use compost directly from the bin applied over the lawn and around the base of plants. You can also use it as a mulch. If you use good garden compost as a mulch or in your general garden culture, you will probably never have a problem with the pH of your soil.

ALKALINE SOIL

In the rare event that your soil tests high on the scale, indicating a soil that is too "sweet," you can quickly bring it back to normal by adding sulfur, iron sulfate (sold as Copperas) or aluminum sulfate, following the directions on the label carefully. But most experienced gardeners find only isolated places where the soil in our part of the country is too alkaline — such as beside concrete driveways which leach lime into the soil, or areas where limestone has been applied incorrectly.

MONTH-BY-MONTH PLANT GUIDE

ORNAMENTAL SHRUBS AND TREES

In this section you will find descriptions of ornamental shrubs and trees from which you can build a beautiful, Southern coastal garden. In addition to the descriptions you will find a month-by-month guide to caring for your plants. The emphasis here is on the ornamental shrubs which will form the backbone of your garden. Although there are relatively fewer trees listed, the ones you'll find described here are some of the best and most well-loved varieties for the Southern garden.

Abelia x grandiflora

Glossy abelia

Of the thirty or so species of abelia, this hybrid is the best for coastal gardens. Its first cousin is abelia 'Edward Goucher', a similar plant that sports a rose-lavender flower.

Often called the "workhorse" of the Southern garden, it's hard to find an old-fashioned home along the southeastern coast of North Carolina without an abelia or two. Once used as a staple for all sorts of garden tasks, some specimen plants can be found in abandoned rural cemeteries, along fence lines and in vacant town lots. Abelias fell into disfavor years ago because they were considered common, but recently they have been rediscovered as extremely durable plants, easily adaptable to our changing weather conditions and as reminders of our heritage. They bloom in the heat of summer, showing a pinkish-white honeysuckle-like flower with little fragrance. They'll tolerate most soil conditions but prefer sandy humus and plenty of sunlight. Prune when they are dormant and have dropped their leaves, or allow your glossy abelia to grow unchecked. Excellent as a foundation material, plant two or three together for a stronger show, or treat them as a hedge or even use them in a mixed bed. You can expect a mature abelia to reach five feet in height and spread to four feet.

MONTH-BY-MONTH GUIDE FOR GLOSSY ABELIA

JANUARY-FEBRUARY	Your plant is dormant.
MARCH	During the winter, your abelia has dropped some foliage. Good garden clean-up is essential this month around the base of the plant and in the flower beds and hedges.
APRIL	You'll start to see some signs of life as your abelia breaks dormancy. Look for small, pale green foliage along the stems and branches. Feed your plant this month with half a cup of Sul-Po-Mag.
MAY	Slugs and snails hide under boards and rocks. At night they'll eat your plants, so treat for them now. Prevent disease by pruning to increase air circulation.
JUNE-AUGUST	The summer months are prime time displays for your abelia. Little care will be needed except to make sure that your plant never wilts.
SEPTEMBER-OCTOBER	Protect from pests and keep your plant clean as dormancy approaches and activity slows.
NOVEMBER-DECEMBER	Prune during this period only, if you choose, but no more than one-third during any one season.

Acer palmatum

Cutleaf Japanese maple

This fascinating small tree is one of the most desirable trees in the coastal landscape because of its interesting foliage, wonderful fall color and amazing summer appearance with deeply serrated foliage and wavy, almost fern-like leaves. Small and slow-growing, these trees rarely exceed twenty feet, though some older cultivars get a little taller. They all offer orange or red fall color, but many cultivars keep a green cast in the leaves even as they change color, so the variegation is intense. There are quite a few cultivated varieties, and the number of folks who grow this tree as a hobby has expanded now to quite a large group. There are specialists who raise the common and very rare hybrids, and the cost per tree can range from a few dollars to several hundred for the more exotic cultivars.

As a species, they are only different from their larger cousins in size and leaf structure, though the characteristics of the maple family are still quite obvious, especially with the strength and durability of the plant, the fall color change and the adaptability to our coastal area. Though they have a few cultural problems, they are quite easy to grow, and should be placed where they can show off their wonderful form. Distinctive and slightly unusual, these trees are valuable additions to any landscape, especially smaller gardens where space is limited.

Any nursery will have them for sale, but you can often find some interesting selections in specialty shops that feature Japanese maples. Grow them in prominent locations which feature well-drained, rich soil. Keep the pH neutral, and give them open sunshine. Avoid fertilizers and pruning. If you can leave the tree alone, you'll have a lasting addition to your garden. Some varieties maintain reddish or copper-colored foliage all season, some change color as the seasons progress. Blight can be a problem, so if the tree becomes affected, spray with a light dose of fungicides, but avoid treating it during the hot days of the summer. There is a type of midge (fly maggot) that attacks the leaves of some trees, as do lace bugs and some other minor pests, all of which can be treated quickly with a basic fruit tree spray applied according to the label directions. Be cautious about using too many pesticides, though, as these trees are somewhat sensitive to chemical applications.

My mother grew her Japanese maple just below her bedroom window so that she could see it every day. Over the years she watched as it matured into a fine tree, and it became one of her favorite garden specialties. She never pruned it, never fertilized it and it was one of the few trees in cultivation that she recommended for every coastal garden.

MONTH-BY-MONTH GUIDE FOR CUTLEAF JAPANESE MAPLE

JANUARY-FEBRUARY	Your tree is dormant. Toward the end of the period, spray the tree and the soil around it with a horticultural oil spray.
MARCH-APRIL	Some new foliage may appear. Protect the tree from wind damage in spring storms, and make sure it is watered. Replace the mulch with clean, dry material.
MAY-JUNE	Full foliage appears and the tree will need some water on a regular basis. Do not fertilize around the base with lawn grass fertilizers.
JULY-AUGUST	You may notice a blight which "scorches" the foliage, shreds the margins of the leaves or discolors the tree in general. Midges may eat the leaves as will lace bugs. Choose a cool day, and late in the evening apply a fruit tree spray according to the label directions. Be careful about drifting spray, and avoid excessive use.
SEPTEMBER-OCTOBER	You will notice some color change as the fall season approaches. Be sure to rake fallen leaves and to keep the base of the tree clean. Continue to water the tree, and do not prune it.
NOVEMBER-DECEMBER	As soon as the tree drops its leaves, check for damaged branches or unwanted growth. Prune very carefully. Cutleaf maples look pretty decorated with lights for the holiday season.

Acer rubrum

Red maple

'Morgan' Often called Morgan's red maple, this is the cultivar for streetside planting because it resists pollution. Orange leaves in the fall.

'October Glory' Perfect for our area, this one gives an intense show of red leaves in autumn.

'Red Sunset' A brilliant show of red leaves in October from a dense growth habit makes this maple perfect for specimen planting. If you choose this one, select an isolated place with lots of room and keep the area clear.

Red maples are the ultimate choice for extra-large shade trees. A quick growth rate, full canopy of leaves and brilliant fall color make this shade tree an American classic. Free of pests, it will tolerate a wide range of soil conditions, but prefers rich, moist, well-drained soil that is slightly acidic. One of the first trees to show flowers and foliage in the spring, it is late to drop leaves in the fall, and holds its autumn color for several weeks. Usually dense, thick and heavily branched, maples provide cool shade, protection for wildlife, wonderful color in the fall, attractive bark and a growth habit that is fast and healthy. You'll get ninety feet of growth with a canopy that exceeds fifty feet. Grow maples in sunny locations.

You can expect four to six feet of growth a year in the first ten years of life, after which growth will slow slightly, though maples tend to expand upward and outward rapidly if they like the conditions. The roots are up at the surface, and they form a dense mat. It's impossible to plant ornamentals beneath them, even in raised bed areas. These roots are vital to the tree's development, and should not be impeded, though a simple ground cover of ivy or vinca may easily enhance the ground level appearance. It's best to leave a maple alone, allowing it to grow and expand at will. Plant it or move it in the dormant season.

Red maples are hallmark trees along the coastal Carolina skyline. Harvested for years for furniture, tools, loom picks and even pulp wood, they are fast growers, quick to recover from storm damage and one of the first trees to appear in cleared landscapes. Though you will probably never live long enough to see a maple reach maturity, it is worthwhile planting this wonderful shade tree, a species that has become well-established in American horticulture for obvious reasons.

MONTH-BY-MONTH GUIDE FOR RED MAPLE

JANUARY	Your maple is dormant.
FEBRUARY	Balmy days may spark some flowers. Look for tight clusters of solid red florets along branches which face southeast.
MARCH- APRIL	Plenty of flowers will show up, along with the seeds which will appear as winged fruits throughout the tree. Maples foliate early in spring, so look for pale green leaves among the limbs. The leaves may appear wilted during warm spring days.
MAY-AUGUST	Growth spurts will push stems, branches and foliage at all levels. Leaves may be red at first, turning to dark green as summer wanes. After the summer solstice, mature branches may become lethargic.
SEPTEMBER	A late growth burst is probable. Fall storms may strip some branches. Take stock of the growth of the tree during the season. It may surprise you.
OCTOBER-NOVEMBER	Show time! By Thanksgiving, your maple will give you all the color and marvelous red-orange display you expect, with brilliant flaming leaves followed by sudden leaf drop.
DECEMBER	Prune the tree as needed.

Aspidistra elatior

Cast Iron Plant

You'll need cool, humus-enriched soil and a shady spot to grow this ornamental. If you have such a space, there is no ground cover which can offer as many advantages. Thick, tough leaves are elongated and up to a foot long with rich, dark green, shiny appearance. The plant spreads quickly by rhizomes just under the soil surface, so water is especially important during dry periods.

Don't look for flowers on this plant because they are very simple and not worth noting. But when all other ground covers are in deep dormancy for the winter, or may have trouble with the summer heat, your cast iron plant will be fresh and upright.

Slugs may damage the leaves, so treat with DE at the first sign. If you live in an area that has extra-hard water, you'll notice iron bacteria stains on the foliage. These stains resemble an oil sheen on the leaf's surface. Simply spray the foliage with a mild (one percent) bleach solution. The healthier the soil, the healthier your aspidistra will be, so keep the nutrition levels high with an annual application of compost.

MONTH-BY-MONTH GUIDE FOR CAST IRON PLANT

JANUARY	Though dormant, your plant will remain green and thick this month. Protect the clumps from cold winter blasts which will kill the plants if they get below 25 degrees for longer than several hours.
FEBRUARY-MARCH	Now is a good time to replace the mulch. Cover the base of the plants with an inch or two of compost.
APRIL	As spring comes early to the region, you'll notice some new growth in the plants. A dose of tankage at the rate of two and a half cups per fifty square feet will guarantee a good start for the season. You may see some flowers close to the ground.
MAY-JULY	Old leaves continue to thrive as new leaves "harden." Notice the dark, shiny appearance of the plant. Use DE to protect from snails and slugs. Late in the summer older foliage may yellow and fade. You can remove these leaves with sharp clippers or shears. If the foliage is discolored by hard water, spray the clump with a bleach solution of one half ounce household bleach per gallon of water. Growth may exceed two feet.
AUGUST-SEPTEMBER	Around Labor Day (not before), you can divide the clump if it is too large for the garden.
OCTOBER-NOVEMBER	Falling leaves from the canopy above your plants may cover them too much. Use a blower to keep the aspidistra clean. Falling debris, pine cones and limbs may damage the plants in fall storms, so protect them.
DECEMBER	Mulch the plants and protect them from winter freezes.

Aucuba japonica

Japanese aucuba

'*Crotonifolia*' This is the male plant needed for producing red fruit on the female varieties. This variegated cultivar is widely produced as a regional favorite.

'*Gold Dust*' Plenty of gold speckles make this aucuba very popular. This is the female plant you will need to produce red fruits in the late summer to fall.

Aucubas are grown for their foliage and fruit, but mostly for the lush, full habit they develop in the garden. Along walls or fences, in mixed beds or group plantings, aucubas have a dense crown with lots of foliage. You can purchase solid green varieties that are either male or female, or you can grow the variegated types with brilliant, golden-spotted and speckled leaves. Remember to purchase both sexes so you'll have red berries. Aucubas grow well in dense shade and will tolerate brighter areas, but direct sun tends to weaken them. The soil should be well-drained, but rich humus or heavily enriched soils are not necessary. These plants can sometimes be temperamental and will develop problems with no warning. Nematodes attack their roots, and bacterial wilt will destroy plants quickly by wilting them to the ground. Otherwise, no special care is needed, and you will be able to enjoy your plant for many years. Aucubas grow upward to four feet and expand to three feet around.

MONTH-BY-MONTH FOR JAPANESE AUCUBA

JANUARY	Birds will build nests in the thick undergrowth of your dormant plant.
FEBRUARY	Examine your plant for problems which include sooty mold, freeze damage and unwanted growth.
MARCH-APRIL	Prune anytime during this period. The shrub will become thick and dense if you prune selected shoots hard in the spring. Allowing your plant to go unpruned will encourage leggy, floppy growth, especially if your aucuba is grown in shade. To prevent problems, use sharp, clean shears to make flat, straight cuts just above axial growth.
MAY	Replace the mulch with clean, dry material. If your plant is weak, fertilize with one cup of tankage or bloodmeal and a half a cup of Epsom salts. Tankage is an organic source of nitrogen, and is the result of the tanning process. It is sold in lawn and garden centers under several brand names, but can be found easily if you ask for it by its generic name.
JUNE-SEPTEMBER	Normal care now during the hot and dry spells of summer and early fall. Do not let your plant dry out. Aucubas root easily, and now is the time to start new plants.
OCTOBER-DECEMBER	Red berries will attract birds

Betula nigra

River birch

A drive through the countryside and farmlands of coastal Carolina, especially a drive that crosses creek beds and streams, will show you lots of river birches. They are often called red birches. This is a species that has about fifty cousins, and it's been hybridized a few times. The result is 'Heritage', a tree among trees, with dark green foliage and shaggy reddish bark, the sure sign that it is a member of the birch family. But if you settle on the species tree for your place you'll do just fine, because it's hard to tell the difference between a hybrid tree and the one that has become famous in residential and commercial landscapes. It weeps a little which adds to the aesthetics. It foliates early in the spring and has delightful fall color. The bark of the tree is shaggy, often curling away from the main trunk in sheets. So, in winter, a good sized river birch will add lots of texture to the garden. It has a few pests like sawfly larvae which strip

the foliage, and it doesn't live long when compared to other trees. But when planted in clusters and clumps it can make a

wonderful addition to your landscape because of its prolific heart-shaped foliage, tremendous growth habit and arching canopy. It will take a partially shaded location, wet soil and an isolated spot to make it grow at its best, and you will be more than pleased with its performance. A healthy tree will reach eighty feet over the years with a spread of thirty feet.

A well-respected American favorite, the river birch is an excellent choice for a corner of the foundation, or a specimen tree planting in your landscape.

MONTH-BY-MONTH GUIDE FOR RIVER BIRCH

JANUARY	Your tree is dormant, but now is a good time to check for storm-damaged limbs or branches that are unwanted.
FEBRUARY-MARCH	You might notice some water flowing from the ends of the branches anytime now as spring approaches. Pools of sap or staining in areas around the base of the tree are common.
APRIL-MAY	The leaves are forming, appearing as reddish or wine-colored whorls along the branches. A late freeze may nip the foliage, but will not cause major damage.
JUNE	The larvae of flies will eat the leaves, often stripping entire branches. If the loss is twenty percent or less, you should not be concerned. Otherwise, a spray-over of Dipel will solve the problem.
JULY-SEPTEMBER	Birches lose leaves early, so a few yellow or brown leaves lost in a fall storm are quite normal.
OCTOBER-DECEMBER	Full color change and leaf loss takes place, and you can prune any time after Thanksgiving, especially lower branches and limbs. By pruning the lower part of the tree you will be making it easier to grow shrubs and ground covers underneath it next year.

Buddleia davidii

Buddleia, Butterfly bush

'Black Knight'   Deep purple, highly fragrant flowers from lance-shaped foliage. Blooms well into fall.

'Nanho Blue'   The standard, old South buddleia, all-purpose, fast-growing with lots of bluish-purple spikes. The plant sometimes dies for no apparent reason.

'Pink Charm'   The pink version of 'Nanho Blue'. A durable shrub with slightly smaller spikes. Highly fragrant.

Buddleias are one of the most popular perennial shrubs in the Southern garden. Though there are about a hundred species, look for the established cultivars. Frequently called butterfly bush, these highly fragrant, arching, mounded shrubs attract songbirds, hummingbirds and butterflies throughout a long growing season that begins in early summer and ends at frost. Native to China, buddleias are old-fashioned Southern favorites that have recently reappeared as excellent, widely adaptable plants. For maximum display, feature your buddleia in a sunny spot with rich, well-drained soil. Group several together for a full arching group effect.

Buddleias grow rapidly and will reach six to eight feet with a spread of four feet. Planted as a cluster, slightly larger mounds can be created.

MONTH-BY-MONTH GUIDE FOR BUDDLEIA

JANUARY	Your plant is dormant. Do you see some gray-green leaves? This is a sign your plant is vigorous, but if a freeze kills some above ground parts, simply cut them back; chances are good the plant will survive.
FEBRUARY	Prune this month. You can reduce your plant by as much as you like. Some gardeners take them back to twelve inches every year, others reduce them by a third or so and allow them to grow as much as six feet.
MARCH-APRIL	Your plants are breaking dormancy now as spring approaches. Notice some leaf development, new sprouts and renewed vigor, all signs of spring push. Fertilize in mid-April with a handful of 5-10-10 fertilizer and a quarter-cup of superphosphate.
MAY	Some spikes begin to form, and the plant will bloom soon. On the last day of the month, fertilize again with a light application of 5-10-10. Apply an inch or so of fresh compost around the base of the plant and mulch the plant.
JUNE-AUGUST	Show time for your buddleia. During this period your plant will perform at its peak. Summer sunshine encourages blooming. Shaded plants produce smaller spikes. Flowers are thrown on each branch, even those that are pinched back after flowering. Nodding spikes from five to twelve inches are common. Water is essential, especially for container grown plants.
SEPTEMBER-OCTOBER	Normal maintenance now as flowering slows. Since the summer solstice, the plant has been getting less active and now shows signs of getting "sleepy." No more fertilizers.
NOVEMBER-DECEMBER	Flowering stops and your plant goes into dormancy for the winter. Protect your plant from winter storms and direct salt spray. During dry periods, water deeply.

Buxus microphylla

Little leaf box, Japanese boxwood

The genus *Buxus* contains only two species that are commonly grown as ornamental shrubs. But from these two species, hundreds of cultivated varieties have become popular as landscape plants in Southern gardens. Over the years, these cultivated varieties have become very confused, so much so that even experienced horticulturists have difficulty classifying the various varieties into recognized groups, much less adopting a uniform terminology. This species, *microphylla*, is a well known species. Often called Japanese boxwood, it is easily recognized by its alternate leaves, rounded growth habit, small height and superb growth rate in the summer. An excellent variety, 'Green Pillow' is common but often difficult to identify. Any good nurseryman will be able to show you this species plant by the recognized name, Little leaf box, but a good indicator is a well-rounded shrub with alternate, rounded leaves. It grows in any soil but can be fickle. So, keep its shallow roots cool with plenty of mulch, go easy on fertilizers, keep the soil well-drained , and grow your Japanese boxwood in partial shade. The more shady the location, the more your plant will "stretch" with greater distance between the nodes. But, in any event, it will work well as a hedge, as a foundation plant or massed in a group bed. Somewhat susceptible to nematodes and animal markings, it is usually free from pests. You can expect the plant to grow as high as five feet if left unpruned, and it will easily spread to four feet.

MONTH-BY-MONTH GUIDE FOR JAPANESE BOXWOOD

JANUARY	Your plant is dormant. Notice some pale foliage, copper-colored leaves and general weakness
FEBRUARY	Replace the mulch this month and keep your plant safe from freezing around the base.
MARCH-APRIL	With good weather your plant may show some signs of growth. As animals begin to patrol out of doors, keep an eye out for those that "mark" your plants. A basic pepper spray or chemical animal repellent will keep them away from prized plants.
MAY-JUNE	Aggressive terminal growth begins now as spring and summer get underway. Plan now for future growth and how your plant will spread and grow within its limits. Now is a good time to open the canopy above your plants to increase sunlight.
JULY-AUGUST	Get a soil test. The pH is important, and will indicate how well your plant will absorb nutrients later in the year. An ideal pH is 6.5 to 7.0. Adjust accordingly so that your boxwood will get full advantage from the soil. Prune at will, especially to shape your plant as you see fit. The fine cuttings can be rooted for other plantings.
SEPTEMBER	If the soil test so indicates, amend the soil this month before Labor Day.
OCTOBER-NOVEMBER	Apply a single dose of Epsom salts around the base of each plant at the rate of one-quarter cup for each foot of growth, mixed with one-quarter cup borax per plant.
DECEMBER	Dormancy begins, and you may see some pale foliage as winter sets in. Harvest a handful or two of tips for holiday decorations, and take a small garbage bag full to your local florist or craft maker to make a seasonal wreath for the door or wall.

Buxus sempervirens

American boxwood

'*Suffruticosa*'   This is the famous dwarf boxwood used for edging. Short and robust, this variety is the classic colonial home boxwood, so popular in the gardens of Williamsburg and other early American settings.

As you will see from reading about *Buxus microphylla*, boxwoods are confusing, because there are so many cultivated varieties from which to choose. It's remarkable that from the two species of boxwoods grown for cultivation, we have hundreds of varieties. The common thread among all is the thick, lush growth, and these characteristics are not lost in American box. But like Japanese boxwood, this plant is fickle. It, like its first cousin, is often difficult to grow. Homeowners complain of severe chlorosis with this species, and the chlorosis often seems to take hold for several years. More than likely, this yellowing of the foliage and general lack of vigor is due to a marked pH imbalance, and the condition can quickly be overcome with proper soil amendments.

Read the section on *B. microphylla* for a good reference, but keep in mind that *B. sempervirens* is more compact, has thicker foliage, often grows tall and erect and is susceptible to many pests. Nematodes attack the roots, animals may mark the plant causing severe burns, and parts of the plant may suddenly expire without an apparent cause. But despite the problems, American boxwood is a garden classic here in the South, and it can easily become a featured part of your garden.

Grow it in partial sun or shade, in well-drained normal garden soil with a neutral pH and a minimum amount of fertilizers. Too much feeding can create problems. Some horticulturists say that the plant tolerates shearing, but I recommend that you leave this plant alone, allowing it to expand to its full potential. It often reacts poorly to pruning, never replacing the branches that are taken away.

This is not a specimen plant, and should be planted with a companion or two, used as a hedge or located on a corner of the foundation. Watch it carefully each season and go after problems aggressively!

An unpruned plant will reach eight feet with a spread of three feet.

MONTH-BY-MONTH GUIDE FOR AMERICAN BOXWOOD

JANUARY	Your plant is dormant. Notice some copper-colored leaves and general weakness.
FEBRUARY	Replace the mulch this month, and keep your plant safe from freezing around the base.
MARCH-APRIL	With good weather, your plant may show some signs of growth. As animals begin to patrol out of doors, keep an eye out for those that "mark" your plants. A basic pepper spray or the chemical "Repel" will help keep them away from prized plants.
MAY-JUNE	Aggressive terminal growth begins now as spring and summer get underway. Plan now for future growth and how your plant will spread and grow within its limits. Now is a good time to open the canopy above your plants to increase the sunlight.
JULY-AUGUST	Get a soil test. The pH is important, and will indicate how well your plant will absorb nutrients later in the year. An ideal pH is neutral 7.0. Adjust accordingly so your boxwood will get full advantage from the soil.
SEPTEMBER	If the soil test so indicates, amend the soil this month before Labor Day.
OCTOBER-NOVEMBER	Apply a single dose of magnesium sulfate at the rate of one-fourth cup per foot of growth, mixed with one-fourth cup borax per plant, scratched into the soil around the base.
DECEMBER	Dormancy begins now, and you may see some pale foliage as winter sets in. Avoid clipping this plant for holiday foliage.

Camellia japonica

Common camellia

There are thousands of varieties in this very large group of evergreen shrubs. Camellia growers often consider growth habit, foliage type, bloom shape and form, and blossoming time as guidelines for classification. For the novice these can be detailed and often confusing, but, as with any plant in the landscape, you should choose plants according to your own tastes and grow these wonderful Old World classics for your pleasure. It is best to purchase these plants from nursery stock while in bloom so that you can see the flower. Camellias will bloom from late fall through the winter and into spring, all of which are ideal times to buy them. Keep in mind that camellias often have variable colors of flowers on the same plant. Though there is a certain dominant color in most varieties, don't be surprised if your plant throws an occasional mutant flower. The selections listed are but a few of the hundreds from which you can choose, and they represent some of the stunning garden favorites that have gained immense popularity here in the coastal area.

'Lady Vansittart'   An upright plant with unusual foliage, this *C. japonica* has pink-flushed flowers, but often blooms with many self-colored mutations. It's very reliable.

'*Mathotiana*'   Very large flowers from a spreading plant with a velvety crimson color.

'R.L. Wheeler'   A Southern favorite, this robust plant has very large foliage and lots of large rose-pink flowers with well-defined yellow stamens.

'White By The Gate'   Here's the white camellia gardeners can enjoy for a large season. Delicate pure-white flowers from an open shrub that rival any colored blossoms in their class. A sterling example of what camellias should be.

Neutral to slightly acid soil is best for growing camellias, and you will find partial shade is ideal for flowering. Though most are cold hardy, those camellias grown in protected areas are the finest examples. The species is generally pest-free though scale can cause problems as can flower thrips and some fungal diseases. Mottled foliage is a good indicator that a problem is present. A good treatment is is a dose or two of supreme horticultural oil, like Volck or Later's, applied in early fall. The new super-refined horticultural oils are excellent. SunSpray is a popular brand. Fungal diseases are spread through fallen flowers, so good sanitation is your best defense. Prune only to remove unwanted growth or to remove plant parts that are damaged. The best time for this simple task is while the plant is blooming or immediately afterwards. Camellias require little feeding, though a side dressing of Sul-Po-Mag applied in late summer can enhance budding and blooming. The southeast part of North Carolina is home to some wonderful varieties and growers of fine camellias and has yielded several presidents of the American Camellia Society. An annual camellia show held each February offers the public a display of thousands of blooms.

Mature camellia plants can exceed twelve feet in height, but rarely grow more than ten feet tall in ideal situations. Since they have a columnar growth habit, they will usually remain within a three- or four-foot radius.

MONTH-BY-MONTH GUIDE FOR CAMELLIAS

JANUARY	Some flowers may fail to open in very cold weather.
FEBRUARY	As temperatures moderate toward the end of the month, more blooming takes place. Prune if need be. Keep the base of the plant clean and free from spent blooms.
MARCH-APRIL	Peak blooming quickly ends as hot weather approaches, and notice some new growth as the terminals of the branches begin to sprout.
MAY-JUNE	A crucial time for good development of your plant for the following season's growth. Buds are being set. Do not prune. Have your soil tested, and adjust the pH as needed. Late in June, apply a cup or so of 5-10-10 fertilizer and an equal amount of superphosphate.
JULY-SEPTEMBER	Water is essential. You can take some cuttings anytime, and around Labor Day feed your plant with a cup of Sul-Po-Mag. Late this month spray your entire shrub with a horticultural oil spray.
OCTOBER-NOVEMBER	Watch for a few blooms as the season approaches. Early varieties will show lots of color.
DECEMBER	Enjoy your plant as it begins to bloom.

Camellia sasanqua

Sasanqua

'Shi Shi Gashira'   Light pink flowers and a spreading habit create the perfect sasanqua for our area. Spreads out rather than growing tall.

'Sparkling Burgundy'   Deep rose-red flowers last a long time. Fragrant and very prolific, this plant spreads out and grows upright to form an exceptional specimen.

'Konjiro' Darker pink flowers form an upright plant that takes the heat and sun. An old favorite for corners of the foundation.

'Yuletide'   Deep red flowers with pronounced stamens bloom slightly later than others.

Sasanquas may be the oldest cultivated plant in our coastal gardens. With azaleas, they were the first to attract the attention of Southern homeowners as early as 1750, and came to the colonies via England. A first cousin to tea (*Camellia sinensis*), sasanquas were traded to the English instead of tea when the astute Chinese realized the British were trying to raise tea in their own hothouses. The plant was worthless as a brew, but the flowers were so striking that a brisk trade developed among ornamental traders. The result, of course, is the great volume of sasanqua cultivars.

There may be a thousand cultivars, many of which are known only in China and Japan. Most are dense, fast-growing and upright, though some sasanquas have a spreading, arching growth habit. All are evergreen, and few exceed ten feet. The majority of the varieties bear white, highly fragrant cup-shaped flowers, though some types have semi-double blooms in pink, red and rose-red colors. These colored blooming plants seem to be the most popular in the coastal southeast, though the white-flowered varieties are quite striking.

Sasanquas grow well in many conditions, as evidenced by the countless specimen plants in historic communities, older residential areas and historic cemeteries. Look for superb examples throughout the area, even in places you wouldn't expect. A sunny place, well-drained soil and rich humus with slightly acid pH will guarantee an excellent site for good performance. Not for nothing did Jim Ferger once call the *Camellia sasanqua* the queen of the Southern coastal garden!

MONTH-BY-MONTH GUIDE FOR SASANQUAS

JANUARY	Your sasanqua has either completed its bloom cycle or is winding down now as winter approaches.
FEBRUARY	Blooming is complete. Your plant is dormant.
MARCH	Dormancy continues. Water your plant and protect it from windy weather, falling limbs and powered lawn and garden tools.
APRIL	Notice some new growth as spring break causes your plant to push new leaves.
MAY	New growth is obvious now as your sasanqua produces bright green leaves. Water regularly and apply a single feeding of 6-6-12 premium fertilizer.
JUNE-AUGUST	Growing is slowed now as the summer develops. Lace bugs, beetles and leaf galls may appear, but will cause no real problem. Fertilize your plant with a handful of Sul-Po-Mag scratched into the soil around the base of the plant on the last day of August.
SEPTEMBER	Water weekly for one-inch accumulation, and replace the mulch with clean, dry material.
OCTOBER-DECEMBER	Your plant will bloom now as fall gets underway.

Cercis canadensis

Eastern redbud, Judas tree

Though some redbuds will grow to thirty feet, most top out between twelve and twenty feet. This makes them ideal for the smaller gardens so popular today. Look at all the advantages that this tree offers: Quick bloom, often well before other spring trees show color, a rich, cerise-colored flower that has a lilac-colored tint, plenty of heart-shaped leaves which offer excellent shade, easy maintenance and pruning if needed, nice yellow fall color and quick raking of fast-falling leaves, plenty of flat, bean-like pods for the birds and a stark, multi-branching display on the winter skyline.

It gets its name from an ancient legend that Judas Iscariot hanged himself from the tree, and thus the tree became cursed, never to grow to soaring heights and destined to be short lived. Cursed or not, both are true. Fifteen years may be all the tree lasts, suddenly dying for no apparent reason. But while you have it in your garden, you are bound to enjoy this wonderful old favorite.

Some nurseries sell white and pink cultivars, but the species tree is a superb choice, never a challenge and always a fine specimen.

MONTH-BY-MONTH GUIDE FOR REDBUD

JANUARY-FEBRUARY	The dormant tree has a lot of branches, aesthetically pleasing in the winter landscape. Late in the period, take a few branches for forcing. Cut well-budded stems, place them in vases of deep, warm water and keep them in a cool, dark place for several weeks. Flowers will appear in early March.
MARCH	Notice some buds swelling along the branches. A flower or two late in the month will kick off the blooming cycle, and any warm day will bring masses of lilac-tinted flowers along southeast facing branches.
APRIL	Well before the other trees, your redbud will throw flowers. The push will continue into the second week of the month and leaves will form rapidly.
MAY	Full canopy will develop now as all flowering is gone. Prune now if needed; otherwise, let the tree fully develop to its potential.
JUNE-SEPTEMBER	The tree is maintenance-free and has no pests, though you may want to increase the bloom potential by fertilizing with a cup or two of superphosphate around the drip line. Make sure the tree is well watered during dry periods.
OCTOBER	Yellow leaves are easy to rake as they fall. The fruit is obvious in the form of pea-like pods filled with several hard, round "peas." You can take a few of these and sow them into a seed bed for later germination.
NOVEMBER	Color change is complete, leaf loss is about over, and you can prune unwanted or damaged wood.
DECEMBER	Clean up around the base of the dormant tree, and see through the branches to the areas above your tree. Now is a good time to open these areas to allow sunlight and air circulation to reach your redbud.

Chaenomeles Speciosa

Flowering quince

'*Moerloosi*'   White flowers flushed with pink make this plant the most popular of the species, but it can be tough to find.

'*Simonii*'   A very popular hybrid, this quince shows lots of double, deep red flowers.

'*Nivalis*'   Pure white flowers on dark green foliage. A genuine garden beauty!

'Spitfire'   Bright red flowers and upright stems.

'Cameo'   Flower form like '*Simonii*', but rich pink instead of red.

'Texas red'   Not as red as 'Spitfire', but a good performer.

There are lots of cultivars from which to choose because this ornamental has been highly developed. It blooms early, often before any other plant in the garden. After a cold winter (which seems to enhance its potential) it is quite a welcome sight as the flowers cover the thorny branches. They begin as tight white or pinkish buds but open on sunny days in early spring to full, semi-double or fully-double large flowers which last several weeks. These East Asian natives are often grown for hedges, and can be clipped, but they are always best left alone, cultivated as specimen plants. They will grow easily in just about any soil, but it is important to place them where they can be fully appreciated from a southeastern window and a clear spot so your neighbors can see them grow.

The early spring bloom is magnificent, and later in the summer you'll find some hard, apple-like fruits on the bush. Though mostly inedible, they are aromatic, and some folks, especially old-timers, enjoy making a tasty preserve from the interesting balls. An unchecked quince will grow to eight feet with a spread of six feet or more. Control its growth by pruning shortly after blooming.

MONTH-BY-MONTH GUIDE FOR FLOWERING QUINCE

JANUARY	Your quince is dormant.
FEBRUARY	Just after the fifteenth of the month, scratch one-quarter cup of bonemeal into the soil around the base of the plant.
MARCH	Some light foliage may appear, but early in the month you'll notice plenty of buds swelling along the branches. Blooming can take place any time.
APRIL	Blooming stops and flowers fade, followed by a flush of new foliage. Prune at will, but be careful not to destroy the basic shape of the plant. Quinces recover quickly from pruning, but don't be too heavy-handed.
MAY-JULY	Summer produces some new growth, but the heat of the dog days will slow the plant's output. Replace the mulch, and be careful working around the plant because of the thorny branches. Don't let the the plant dry out.
AUGUST-OCTOBER	Pests will not be a problem. Now is a good time to open the canopy of plants above your quince.
NOVEMBER	If you have not done so already, harvest the fruits.
DECEMBER	You can harvest a few selected branches this month through the remainder of the winter for forcing indoors. Quinces force easily. Take long, budded branches and place them in deep vases of warm water. A sunny spot near a heat source will cause the flowers to open indoors during the holidays and into late winter.

Cornus florida

Dogwood

This species is the king of the flowering native trees, and in its pure state, there is none more spectacular. Often seen along rural roadsides, forest traces and woodland borders, the beauty of the dogwood in spring is incredible. No wonder it is North Carolina's state tree.

In cultivation, it can be equally impressive. A variety named *'Pleniflora'* produces extra large, pure white blossoms from a weeping tree. *C. florida rubra* has blush-pink petals while 'Cherokee Chief' has deep, rose-red flowers. There are quite a few cultivars, most of which grow well here. Another species, *C. kousa*, is gaining popularity as a wonderful dogwood for our area.

Dogwoods are the majestic beauties of our coastal environment. When so many native trees are being replaced by developed sites and hybrid "wonder trees" have become so popular, an old-fashioned dogwood is a wonderful reminder of our area's botanical heritage, Southern charm and natural beauty. Choose a sunny spot which will allow your tree to grow and expand at will. Dogwoods grow upward and outward and need good air circulation. Well-drained soil is a must, and *C. florida* does not tolerate wet feet or drought conditions. At maturity. the tree will reach fifty feet with a spread of forty feet or more. Whether used as specimen trees, natural plantings or at the corners of the foundation, they deserve a premium location where they can easily become the featured part of your landscape.

But they require some specific care to guarantee their good health and vigor. Protect your trees from needless injury and borer attacks by keeping garden equipment away from them. Bumps, nicks and cuts from mowers, bicycles and tools can often lead to open wounds which breed trouble. The hot, humid weather of the coastal plain causes septoria leaf spot, ascochyta blight and mildew, all of which can diminish a dogwood's bloom potential. If you follow the month-by-month guide, especially while your tree is young, you can avoid many of the problems now faced by flowering dogwoods. Initial soil preparation and site selection are important considerations.

Dogwoods dug from the wild are not reliable trees, and do not transplant very well, so it's always in your best interest to purchase your tree from a nursery or garden center.

MONTH-BY-MONTH GUIDE FOR DOGWOOD

JANUARY	A few red berries persist on the dormant tree. Prune any branches or limbs as needed. Look for obvious signs of winter damage.
FEBRUARY-MARCH	Get ready for spring flowering by observing as your tree's buds begin to swell. Look for purple-colored flower buds along the branches. Spray the entire tree—trunk and branches—with dormant horticultural oil spray.
APRIL	Flowering can take place at any time. Petals will appear discolored at first, purple, yellow or red, but will open to the typical creamy-white flowers so easily recognized. Take extra care to protect the tree from injury. Wrap the trunks of younger trees with a commercial tree wrap if you think damage may take place.
MAY	Clean up beneath the base of the tree, rake away old mulch, and inspect the trunk for insects. If you see pin holes or sawdust discharge, spray the entire tree with horticultural oil spray or a commercial fruit tree spray. Avoid spraying young foliage. The tree will show full foliage by the end of the month.
JUNE	As soon as the new leaves have "hardened," spray the tree with commercial fruit tree spray for a second application if you still notice signs of pests.
JULY-SEPTEMBER	Water is essential. Since dogwoods do not tolerate drought, apply half an inch of water every three days. Protect your tree from injury, and avoid lawn grass fertilizers in the root zone. Mulch around the base.
OCTOBER	Apply a quarter cup of Sul-Po-Mag per inch of tree trunk diameter around the base of the tree and water well. Your tree may have some color change and leaf loss. Red berries are obvious as the autumn season arrives. Fall storms may damage some limbs, so be prepared.
NOVEMBER	Apply a fresh layer of mulch. Brilliant fall color takes over as your tree shows rich red and burgundy colors. Around Thanksgiving, most leaves are falling and red berries appear on the grey-white branches. Check the tree for storm damage, obvious signs of injury or borers.
DECEMBER	Your tree is dormant. Harvest some of the lower branches for holiday decorations, especially those with lots of red berries. Wildlife will enjoy the fruit as well.

Cortaderia Selloana

Pampas grass

'Silver Comet'   We see this variety quite frequently used as a massed planting. It's the most popular of the two main varieties, but may not offer as much show as the other.

'Sunningdale Silver'   The plumes of this one have more sheen, and tend to be more feathery. Not as readily available as 'Silver Comet'.

The genus has only one species, and in the grass family, this is a bit uncommon. Nonetheless, pampas grass is quite popular, both as a specimen and as a massed planting. There are both male and female plants, the female having more show from its plumes than the male plant. So, try to specify which you want, though you may not be assured of getting it.

This very common grass is seen in residential plantings, commercial sites and industrial areas, simply because it covers vast areas, will grow to a good height and is an excellent plant for any specific, sunny spot in a large landscape. In a corner of a rolling lawn, as part of a natural massed bed or along a fence line, it can be an attractive plant. It's pest-free, requires little maintenance and virtually no cultivation. The plant spreads more than it grows to be tall. Six feet of top growth is about all it will gain, and it can expand much further as it matures.

Sunny locations are best in just about any soil type. The plant is a strong perennial and expands yearly with new growth which replaces last year's mound. The plumes are borne in late summer and persist 'til late autumn. The plumes become "ratty" in winter and should be pruned back. The entire plant looks unkempt when it's in dormancy, so a clean, clear reduction down to the ground is best in early winter. The leaves are hard to cut, tough and razor sharp, so be careful when handling it.

If you have to fertilize it, you have a sickly plant that probably can't be helped, though most folks who plant pampas grass in the lawn areas of their landscapes inadvertently feed the plant when they fertilize their lawns.

Some simple manicuring and common sense grooming will help this plant grace your landscape.

MONTH-BY-MONTH GUIDE FOR PAMPAS GRASS

JANUARY	Your plant is dormant. Some leaves are still gray-green, and by this time you should have pruned most of the plant back to within a foot or so of the ground.
FEBRUARY-MARCH	Clean up blowing plumes and trim around the base.
APRIL-MAY	New growth appears from outside and the interior of the plant. Water is essential.
JUNE-AUGUST	Heavy growth will develop, especially if the plant is located in your lawn. The long, graceful spike may appear, but plumes are awhile off. Wildlife, bees and yellow jackets may make a home in the dense growth.
SEPTEMBER	Panicles may appear on the spikes. Plumes with feathery flowers and seed heads become more obvious.
OCTOBER-NOVEMBER	Full blooming takes place now as the plant reaches full maturity. Some foliage fades.
DECEMBER	As soon as winter winds desiccate the plant, prune it back and clean it up for a neater appearance.

x Cupressocyparis leylandii

Leyland cypress

This tree is a hybrid cross between several genera and was discovered in England in the late 1800s. It made its way into the coastal area of the Southeast only recently, however, but has quickly become a very popular tree. Used as a screen, hedge or specimen planting, Leyland cypress is fast-growing, dense and thick and can often reach one hundred feet at maturity.

The foliage is dark green, flat and scale-like and has a spiraling growth habit around the branches. It makes the perfect 'Christmas Tree' because of its conical shape and rich color, but the main trait of the Leyland is its remarkable growth rate. You can expect six feet or more per year from a young plant.

There are several cultivars with various foliage types and colors, but the species plant is well recognized as the Leyland for coastal gardens. Grow it in well-drained soil only, full sun locations and make sure the young trees are well supplied with rich humus and water. Sweet soil does not suit the plant well, but acid conditions are equally harmful, so keep the pH neutral. Avoid pruning your tree, and make sure it is planted in a place where it can reach its full potential without pruning or moving. Treat bagworms quickly as they pose a serious threat.

MONTH-BY-MONTH GUIDE FOR LEYLAND CYPRESS

JANUARY	Your dormant tree is one of the few dark green, fully foliated trees in the winter landscape.
FEBRUARY-MARCH	Test the soil and maintain a constant neutral pH. Replace the mulch and water well during dry periods.
APRIL-MAY	New growth can take place anytime. Look for spiral leaves encircling the branches. New growth is pale green above, dark green below.
JUNE-AUGUST	Keep a watchful eye for bagworms, and treat them rapidly with Dipel. Be persistent and destroy them quickly. If the weather is hot and dry, make sure the tree has enough water.
SEPTEMBER-NOVEMBER	Normal maintenance now through the fall, and now is a good time to evaluate your tree's performance, relocate it if need be or add other plants close by.
DECEMBER	Add some lights to your Leyland during the holidays as it makes the perfect "season's greetings" tree.

Daphne Odora

Winter daphne

!ALL PARTS OF THIS PLANT ARE POISONOUS!

Of all the coastal Carolina plants, this one may give you the most pleasure and the most challenge. Expensive, hard to find and fickle, winter daphne is a puzzler. It often dies for no apparent cause, and at other times it tolerates the worst of conditions, throwing large clusters of flowers from vigorous plants. But for all the trouble, the fragrance is so intense and so delightful in the otherwise dormant garden, it's worth it to try your hand at daphne despite all its problems. If you plant it in well-drained, sweet soil and don't attempt too much cultivation you should be able to enjoy your daphne for several years.

Choose the location wisely because daphne is hard to move once established. Pruning should not be done, and if parts of the plant fail, simply remove them without pruning other parts. Sunshine is needed for good blossoming, but partial shade is quite acceptable. From the first signs of flowering in late winter through a long bloom period that lasts into spring, you'll notice the fragrance of this wonderful plant, recognizing it as one of the most sought after and prized fragrances in all the world's gardens.

A healthy daphne will grow to be four feet tall, and may spread over five feet, but the average plant is a little less in size.

MONTH-BY-MONTH GUIDE FOR WINTER DAPHNE

JANUARY	Flower buds can appear at any time, and though they might not open for weeks, the slightly purple color will become more obvious.
FEBRUARY-MARCH	Watch for flowers any time as the plant throws clusters of pink-purple, highly fragrant blossoms.
APRIL	A few blossoms may persist, but the plant will appear dormant as most flowering ceases.
MAY	New foliage pushes through the terminal buds . A very light application of 6-6-12 will enhance growth.
JUNE-SEPTEMBER	Plenty of water, no more feeding and light mulching are all you need to do. Be careful not to bump the plant or otherwise scar it as you mow, trim weeds and cultivate the summer garden.
OCTOBER-DECEMBER	Adequate water is a half an inch every three days, but you may need more if it's really dry. Don't disturb the roots and try to leave the plant alone.

Deutzia Gracillis

Slender deutzia

Alice B. Russell

Of the classic Southern landscape plants, slender deutzia is one of the favorites. Though they stand alone as excellent featured ornamental plants, deutzias perform well as hedges and are always best unsheared and left alone. If you plant your deutzia in a shrub border you'll have many years of maintenance-free beauty. Small leaves, large clusters of small white flowers and a long-lasting bloom habit make this ornamental a wonderful choice for the spring flower bed. The plant will grow to five feet and probably won't exceed three feet in width, but it usually maintains a slightly smaller growth habit with just light pruning. Long, slender branches can become dense with foliage as the summer progresses, and you should prune it as soon as it finishes blooming so you'll have lots of flower clusters for next spring. The flowers last a long time though they are not fragrant. When most other early spring bloomers have dropped their flowers, your deutzia will still be quite lovely. Plenty of sunshine, well-drained neutral soil with a good humus content will enhance the dense upper level root system, and don't worry about pests because your slender deutzia is a hardy, strong contender!

Alice B. Russell

MONTH-BY-MONTH GUIDE FOR SLENDER DEUTZIA

JANUARY	Look for tan-colored stems with obvious bud eyes and no leaves as your plant sleeps through the remaining winter months
FEBRUARY-MARCH	Apply a handful of phosphate around Valentine's Day and apply some fresh mulch. As March winds approach, make sure your plant is watered well.
APRIL	Foliage appears before the flowers, but some small clusters of flower buds can show up anytime.
MAY	Blooming comes early and lasts a long time.
JUNE	Prune and shape this month as needed.
JULY-SEPTEMBER	Though your plant will have no serious pests, watch for weeds that harbor beetles and a few caterpillars which can be controlled with Dipel dust. Around Labor Day scratch a handful or two of bonemeal around the base of the plant.
OCTOBER-DECEMBER	Make sure the plant never dries out. A good fall mulch will help preserve good health. If freezing weather and severe winds are a threat, spray with dormant oil.

Eleagnus pungens

Eleagnus, Thorny eleagnus

'*Maculata*' This colorful variety of the species has a broad yellow patch in the center of the leaf. Highly ornamental, this cultivar is somewhat difficult to find.

Here's a classic Southern landscape plant that offers some unusual growth habits. It's a fast grower, often exceeding twelve feet in just a few years. It's thorny, so handle it with caution. The new leaves are borne rapidly on expanding arches in early spring and begin with a buff-colored outer surface which is often silver or copper-colored on the reverse side. Older leaves mature to a gray-silver color in masses along the branches. If left unpruned the plant forms a thick shrub and when used as a hedge will provide excellent protection and privacy. It is used as a screen for swimming pools, tennis courts and recreation areas. It is an excellent plant for borders of parking lots and along the tops of berms. It tolerates salt spray very well. The bloom is a bell-shaped, highly fragrant flower that appears in the fall in unpruned plants. The fruits are fleshy, oval, pink, grape-like drops which are prized by wildlife.

This is an aggressive performer and will require some cultivation, but little else. It's pest-free. Grow this plant only if you want quick, thick coverage.

MONTH-BY-MONTH GUIDE FOR ELEAGNUS

JANUARY-FEBRUARY	Replace the mulch and rake around the base of the dormant plant. Though it's an evergreen, some foliage may fall during the winter. You might notice some new stem growth along the branches.
MARCH	New growth may appear anytime. Look for long, thin sprouts and very small, pale green leaves.
APRIL-MAY	New growth is quite obvious, exceeding several feet in little time. Prune at will to control the size of the plant, or allow it to grow to full potential, depending on the purpose of the plant in the landscape. A flower or two is not uncommon.
JUNE-JULY	Pruning continues as you wish. Thorns are appearing now, so use a pair of leather gloves while working with the branches. Use a forced stream of water to knock out spider webs if they appear, or treat the plant with pyrethrins, depending on the severity of the problem.
AUGUST	More growth and more pruning. You'll be surprised at how much of both! Some flowers may appear. Your plant will tolerate the roughest weather conditions. Drought, winds and hurricanes don't bother this reliable ornamental.
SEPTEMBER	The mature plant has lots of silvery foliage.
OCTOBER	After the plant blooms in early October, grape-like fruits begin to form. Pruning continues as needed.
NOVEMBER	A few yellow leaves appear as dormancy approaches. Though it seems hard to believe, new growth is still coming, and you may have to prune again.
DECEMBER	Small birds find a home in your eleagnus and dormancy brings a quiet time to the plant. Some leaves may fall. On the coldest day of the month, take a good look at your eleagnus. You might be surprised to see yet another new sprout appearing along the branches.

Eriobotrya Japonica

Loquat

This stout, evergreen, bushy tree can reach heights of twenty-five feet with a spread of eight to ten feet if we have several years of mild winters. Most times your loquat will have a few seasons of damaging winters and you can expect your plant to be more shrub-like. A vigorous grower, a loquat reminds us of a viburnum because of the deep green, thickly-veined, large, oblong leaves, perhaps the strongest feature of this Oriental native. Older plants will throw a five-petaled creamy-white flower in the autumn. The plant's wonderful, sweet scent derives from the large clusters of flowers which last well into cooler months. The pear-shaped, orange-colored fruits ripen over a long period of time, and those that survive the winter and wildlife are remarkably good for out-of-hand eating. Unfortunately, fruiting is not a sure thing because of the damage that so often takes place in the winter. So, loquats are generally grown here along our coast for their foliage and dense shrubbiness. For best results, plant yours along a wall on the west or south side of the house, or in a mixed foliage bed that will create a good backdrop. Treat yours as if it were becoming a specimen plant, featured on the corner of the foundation, or up front where folks can appreciate this stately beauty. One of the best known specimen loquats is owned by the Tinga family, and is grown for ornamental purposes at their Castle Hayne, North Carolina, nursery.

MONTH-BY-MONTH GUIDE FOR LOQUAT

JANUARY	Fruits continue to mature as colder days and nights slow growth.
FEBRUARY	Protect your plant from freezing weather if possible, but do not use plastic covers. If bark splitting occurs, prune at once to avoid disease later. On windy days make sure your plant does not become too dry.
MARCH	Your plant is dormant.
APRIL-MAY	Spring break begins and your loquat shows signs of renewed energy. Good garden sanitation and fresh mulch are essential.
JUNE	Watch for Japanese beetles. Treat with pyrethrins and Rotenone, and check often for caterpillars which may eat the leaf margins. Use Dipel to control them. The undersides of newly formed leaves have a brown, fuzzy appearance. Cottony fibers along new stems are normal.
JULY	Fertilize now with a cup of 6-6-12 fertilizer, a half a cup of bloodmeal or tankage and a half a cup of superphosphate. No feeding after August thirty-first.
AUGUST	Your plant will appear to sleep in the summer heat, but much is happening. Good watering is essential as roots are developing and blossom set is taking place.
SEPTEMBER	Check for pests regularly. Water is essential.
OCTOBER-DECEMBER	Watch for blooming during this period.

Fatsia japonica

Fatsia

For shade areas of the garden, not too many plants surpass fatsia. It's an excellent performer. This fast-growing evergreen shrub reaches six feet in just a few short growing seasons and spreads out to six feet in all directions. The leaves are tropical in nature, deeply lobed, deep green and somewhat coarse. They form at the tops of the branches. The plant is deciduous in the spring, losing the last season's foliage as new leaves form in the terminals of the thick stems. The flowers are prominent clusters of creamy-white, ray-like blooms which appear in the fall, and they are an interesting addition to this lush plant. Ideal for the coastal plain, fatsia grows best in slightly acid soil, partial shade and moist soil. Forget maintenance, as pruning and feeding will not be required. A good place for this plant is along the foundation, in a cool corner, or in a mixed natural bed with other shade-loving plants.

MONTH-BY-MONTH GUIDE FOR FATSIA

JANUARY	The dormant plant retains its tropical appearance. Cold winds and exposure may be harmful, so protect the plant from severe weather.
FEBRUARY	Protect from freezing.
MARCH-APRIL	Anytime this period you might notice the lower leaves fading into pale green, then yellow as the season ends for them. Some new growth may appear in the terminals of the branches.
MAY	Lower leaves turn yellow and drop away. New leaves form at the top of the plant.
JUNE	All the foliage is replaced by new growth which expands rapidly. The whole plant grows in all directions.
JULY-AUGUST	Normal care now as your fatsia shows its best appearance during this season. Some slugs may nibble the edges of the leaves and a flower or two may appear.
SEPTEMBER-OCTOBER	As leaves fall from trees and the season changes, you'll be surprised how tropical your plant will remain, a nice reminder of the previous summer season. In fact, fall is when the fatsia puts out its flowers and fruits. The flowers are creamy-white spikes with radiating florets that are unpleasantly scented. Fruit forms after the flowers in the form of green, grape-like pods.
NOVEMBER	For a different holiday decoration, bring some of the leaves indoors for the next week or two.
DECEMBER	Though the foliage remains green, your plant is dormant.

Forsythia x. intermedia

Border forsythia

'*Spectabilis*'   Often called showy border forsythia, this is a dense shrub with a massive blooming habit.

'Beatrix Farrand'   Sparse blossoms along a thick woody stem make this forsythia attractive as a specimen, featured ornamental. This cultivar can also be trained as a hedge.

'Karl Sax'   This popular plant is a dense plant which flowers early. Thick and full, the abundance of flowers makes this plant a brilliant addition to the dormant landscape. 'Karl Sax' has red and purple fall foliage.

Border forsythia often blooms before anything else in the spring garden. It's not uncommon at all to find a few yellow flowers along the bare stems in late winter when all else is fast asleep. Because of its striking yellow color, it is easy to understand why folks plant this early spring beauty where it can be seen from lots of windows! It is a carefree and pest-resistant shrub. There are some examples of forsythia which have never been pruned, though pruning certainly enhances the shape and bloom potential. It is important to prune immediately following flowering and at no other time. Pruning should be done with extra-sharp, clean shears, alternating between outward and inward facing eyes on each branch with the main objective being to eliminate thick, crowded shrub centers, and to reduce the overall size of the plant. Forsythias which stand alone in the open garden can be left to grow at will, but a height of six feet should be maintained. Well-drained, slightly acid soil which has been enhanced with compost is best, and your plant will perform best in bright, sunny areas away from other plants. Forsythias grow wider than taller. A full plant will reach five feet around and up to six feet in height.

MONTH-BY-MONTH GUIDE FOR BORDER FORSYTHIA

JANUARY -FEBRUARY	Though dormant, your plant may throw a bloom or two. Now is a good time to bring a few branches indoors for forcing.
MARCH	Don't be surprised to see your plant burst into full bloom any day. Prune it after it blooms, even while it is blooming if you want flower spikes in the house.
APRIL	Spring break will push your plant into full foliage which requires plenty of water. Mulch the base with fresh pine straw or pine bark.
MAY-JUNE	Feed your plants this period with a cup of Sul-Po-Mag applied at the drip line and scratched into the soil.
JULY-OCTOBER	Your forsythia is maintenance-free, but water is essential for excellent bud set.
NOVEMBER FIRST	Another cup of Sul-Po-Mag around the base will promote better blooming. Now is a good time to move your plant if you wish to.
DECEMBER	Check the nurseries for better values on new plants which make excellent landscape additions this month

Gardenia Jasminoides

Cape jasmine

'*Fortuniana*'   Sometimes called Florida gardenia, this is a frequently sold cultivar. The tight center of the flower opens to a compact bloom that is not as fragile as some suggest.

'Mystery'   The gardenia for containerizing. Smaller and sometimes thicker, the flowers are smaller but equally as fragrant as their larger cousin's. Blooms fade quickly, but the bush is prolific, often throwing a bloom or two as late as September.

'McClelland's 58'   A rare find, but worth the effort in searching. This old cultivar became quite popular in California for producing show grade flowers with large petals and heavy perfume.

Cape jasmine are also named gardenias after Dr. Alexander Garden, the South Carolina botanist who found them in the Cape Colony in the late 1800s. A Southern classic, this plant rivals any offered around the globe for foliage display and bloom habit. They are unmatched for fragrance, and it has been said that the perfume from a few blossoms is as intoxicating as the scent from the entire shrub, which often produces flowers for several weeks during the early summer. Gardenias are considered fragile, but they tolerate a number of conditions well if they are kept in good health. Grow your plant in partial shade for good blooming. As the stems stretch for the light, they produce plants that are slightly more open, and this less dense growth makes for better air circulation as well as slightly larger flowers. Whiteflies are frequent pests which cause a related fungal disease that leaves a sooty, black mold on the foliage and stems. Keep your plant free from whiteflies by running your hand-held vacuum around your plant every day or two and treat your plant with a horticultural oil spray frequently. A mild fungicide will control the soot. Well-drained neutral soil is best for culture, and make sure your plant is well-watered during the summer. A spread of three or four feet and a height of ten feet can be attained in good conditions. The average plant is slightly less in size.

MONTH-BY-MONTH GUIDE FOR GARDENIA

JANUARY	Your plant is dormant. Notice some yellow or pale green foliage. This "chlorosis" is quite normal, and you should not respond to it.
FEBRUARY	Protect from a deep freeze or windy and very cold conditions. Gardenias exposed to weather below 25 degrees will show some damage, often requiring heavy pruning later. Cover with sheets of paper, not plastic. Freezing water, ice or snow will not cause a problem other than excess weight.
MARCH	On the 20th of the month, rake away all mulch and treat the soil around the base of the plant with a half a cup of baking soda, a fourth of a cup of Epsom salts and a fourth a cup of superphosphate. Spread these evenly around the base of the plant and water well. Do not replace the mulch.
APRIL-MAY	Prepare for blooming by watering your plant regularly, protecting it from drying winds and fertilizing with one cup of 6-6-12 fertilizer. Spray the stems, foliage and and trunk with dormant oil spray, making sure the undersides of the leaves are treated as well as other plant parts.
JUNE	Your gardenia will bloom now. Harvest the flowers daily. No feeding and no spraying while it blooms. Deadhead the plant daily (removing spent flowers from the pedicles) and keep the base of the plant clean from dead flowers. Replace the mulch now with clean, dry pine straw or pine bark mulch.
JULY	Any pruning should be done now. Pruning at any other time will decrease flower yield. Whiteflies and other insects may be obvious now, so spraying may be necessary. In severe cases use a chemical insecticide until you gain control, following the label directions carefully.
AUGUST-SEPTEMBER	A good time for stem cuttings to propagate more plants. Gardenias root nicely and will grow rapidly in the off-season. Water now is crucial for good bud set for next season's flowers. Watch for a growth spurt which sometimes lasts until November.
OCTOBER-DECEMBER	Growth will slow now as dormancy begins. Some leaf loss is due to cool weather, and copper-colored leaves or deep purple, pale green foliage is an apparent indication of deep sleep dormancy. Keep your plant clean.

Gardenia jasminoides 'radicans'

Dwarf gardenia

This small version of the great Cape jasmine will offer all the fragrance and charm of the Southern classic gardenia, but on a smaller scale and with a slightly different growth habit. Though it requires the same soil conditions, and has the same water and sunlight requirements as its taller relative, it will perform well as a low border in shady locations, as a miniature hedge by the walkway, or along a wall or stone barrier. It can be containerized for patio or deck plantings and is often seen in massed beds around commercial buildings. Easy to raise and quick to flower, *'Radicans'* is one of the most popular plants in the garden and is readily available. Somewhat susceptible to whitefly and mealybug, affected plants become pale and chlorotic. Black, sooty mold often appears on plants which have been attacked by insects. Since *'Radicans'* is a low grower, treatment and prevention of pests is simple with commercial insecticides. These plants are heavy feeders and will perform best if they have fertilizers several times during the growing season, and you can expect healthy plants to bloom freely during the summer. Plant several together for a thicker appearance. Partial shade is a good growing recommendation.

This plant never exceeds 18 inches in height, but can expand over several feet as it grows into uncrowded spaces.

MONTH-BY-MONTH GUIDE FOR DWARF GARDENIA

JANUARY	Your dormant plant will have some pale, thin leaves.
FEBRUARY	Now is a good time to scatter a handful or two of superphosphate around the base of your plants. Some leaf loss is normal. Protect from severe weather.
MARCH	Late in the month, feed each plant with a half a cup 6-6-12 fertilizer and spray each plant with a horticultural oil spray.
APRIL	Keep a watchful eye for pests and keep your plants weed-free.
MAY-JUNE	Your plants will bloom this period. Old flowers should be picked. Harvest small, fresh blooms for your pleasure, but keep in mind that they will last only a day or so. A hand-held vacuum is good for whitefly control. Water regularly.
JULY-SEPTEMBER	Some foliage loss is normal. Otherwise, healthy plants continue to spread. The summer heat will trigger dormancy, though an occasional flower is likely. Around Labor Day, but no later than the twentieth of the month, fertilize with another application of 6-6-12.
OCTOBER-NOVEMBER	Spray your plants with a horticultural oil spray.
DECEMBER	Protect your 'Radicans' from severe weather.

Hamamelis x intermedia

Witch hazel

The advantage of growing this delightful small tree is the late winter blooming that offers fragrant flowers just before the spring season arrives. But the rest of the year is important too, because witch hazels make ideal trees in the small garden or general landscape for lots of other reasons. Fall color is often brilliant, the plant showing red or orange foliage and lots of seed pods which contain several interesting black seeds. The tree is pest-free and requires little effort, as long as the soil is ordinary and fairly moist, and you can grow your tree in partial shade or open, sunny locations. Mature trees usually reach twenty feet, though a healthy specimen may get a little taller and more full. There are several cultivars available. 'Jelena' has reddish flowers while 'Arnold Promise' is the popular tree in this area offering yellow blooms.

Avoid pruning this tree so you'll have lots of flowers each winter, and it's best to grow it in a place where it can be seen from all sides, either in a spot by itself, or mixed with low-growing shrubs that allow its arching branches to be seen.

Witch hazel is not a common plant, but this wonderful tree should be used in your landscape as a carefree ornamental and interesting addition to the late winter or early spring garden.

MONTH-BY-MONTH GUIDE FOR WITCH HAZEL

JANUARY-FEBRUARY	Though dormant, the tree will bloom on any balmy winter day. Some flowers will appear anytime, while many others will wait until warmer weather. Blooms are long-lasting and fragrant.
MARCH	Blooming may continue through the end of the month. Some foliage may appear.
APRIL-MAY	Leaves appear during this period. Lobed or serrated, they are rich green and wavy. Some flower pods will persist and may split to expose their seeds. Prune now, but avoid excessive cutting so you'll preserve the blooming cycle for next season.
JUNE-AUGUST	Your witch hazel won't be bothered with pests. Test the soil and amend accordingly. Witch hazel grows best in neutral, ordinary soil. Mulch the base of young plants, and don't let the plant dry out.
SEPTEMBER-OCTOBER	Late in the period, you'll notice some color change. The foliage is brilliant in fall. Some flower buds may be obvious along the branches.
NOVEMBER-DECEMBER	Flower buds appear along the bare branches. No pruning, but make sure the plant is watered. Protect your small tree from damaging winds and falling debris. Replace the mulch with clean, dry material. If a deep freeze threatens, protect the young plant.

Hibiscus syriacus

Rose of Sharon, Althea, shrub althea

Alice B. Russell

This close relative of the tropical hibiscus which has become so popular in coastal settings is an ideal choice for the gardens of our area. It will grow in many conditions, often surviving poor soil and neglect. But with just a little care, this plant will give you all the color and display you expect from coastal garden plants, showing tropical-like flowers throughout the summer and into fall.

It's an old-fashioned plant, and was once used as a hedge material, in plantings around out-buildings and as a specimen in the open, rural yard. Over the years, it has become popular in urban gardens because of its tradition and its link to old-South gardens. It's easy to cultivate and you can expect twelve feet of top-growth and a spread of four to six feet.

Partial sun is acceptable, but full sun is better. Slightly acid soil is a good pH, and make sure the plant is protected from severe winds, heavy rain and salt spray. In the natural garden or in small landscapes, it can be a show-stopper when it's in bloom.

Look for the old standby 'Red Heart', a white flower with a red eye. 'Woodbridge' is a large reddish-pink flower and 'Blue Bird' is a beautiful lavender-blue flower. There are many wonderful cultivars with some exciting flowers.

All cultivars in the species are deciduous and are pruned in winter. The flowers are produced on current season's wood.

96

MONTH-BY-MONTH GUIDE FOR ROSE OF SHARON

JANUARY-FEBRUARY	The plant is dormant and has no foliage. If you have not done so, prune the plant before February twentieth.
MARCH	As the soil warms, many plants will break dormancy late in the month. But your Rose of Sharon will "sleep" a little longer than most plants. Resist the urge to fertilize or cultivate around the plant before it comes to life later in the spring.
APRIL	Late in the month, you will see some foliage growing around the stems. The whorls of leaves sprout around the bud eyes along the stems. New growth will also sprout from the ends of the stems where the plant was pruned. Fertilize now with a single application of 6-6-12 fertilizer.
MAY	Growth continues, and the plant will completely leaf out. The flowers may appear as rough, green pods. Water is essential as these buds form.
JUNE-AUGUST	Blooming begins this period with tight buds opening to hibiscus-type flowers. The flowers will last for several days.
SEPTEMBER	Blooming slows during the late summer. Test the soil pH.
OCTOBER	As the days get longer and dormancy approaches, the leaves will turn pale yellow. Some leaf loss occurs. Amend the soil according to the soil test last month.
NOVEMBER-DECEMBER	Dormancy arrives and the plant loses its leaves. Prune now, reducing the plant by no more than one third its original height. Notice the bud eyes. If you want the plant to sprout new growth towards the inside of the plant, thus creating more columnar growth, prune above an inward facing eye. If you want the plant to spread outward, prune above an outward facing eye.

Hydrangea macrophylla

Hydrangea

'Blue Bonnet' (Hortensia type) The old standby of the blue hydrangeas, this vigorous plant produces large, mounded panicles from late spring to mid-summer.

'Blue Wave '(Lacecap)   A rich, purple-blue flower is touched with light blue or white on the outer petals of this classic, delicate plant which is known for its quick green-up in spring and response to fertilizers and soil amenders

This deciduous, bushy shrub is a classic of the Carolina coastal garden. The hortensia types are the most famous, producing the large mophead-like flowers from thick-foliaged plants. The more delicate, light lacecaps have broader, flatter flowers with fertile flowers in the tight center and sterile inflorescenses on the outer bands. The lacecaps are less prominent in the Southern garden, but perhaps more desirable because of the unfamiliar growth habit. In all plants except white varieties, color is determined by soil acidity. A pH of 5.5 or below produces blue or purple flowers. Pink flowers, or in some cases rosy-red blooms are produced in sweeter soil. For best blooming, don't prune more than half the plant each year. Hydrangeas like it moist and cool, and dappled sunlight produces plenty of flowers. Be cautious of direct sunshine.

The height and spread of this plant is determined by pruning. If you prune hard each year, the most it will grow is upward to five feet and five feet around. Lacecaps tend to grow slightly taller and bigger around. If left unpruned, expect six feet in height and spread from either variety.

MONTH-BY-MONTH GUIDE FOR HYDRANGEA

JANUARY	Your plant is dormant.
FEBRUARY	Replace any older mulch with fresh material.
MARCH	Though you cannot see activity, it is beginning as the weather warms. Toward the end of the month, fertilize with with a light dose of 6-6-12 and half a cup of superphosphate per plant.
APRIL	Watch for green-up as spring push begins. Water is important.
MAY	Your plant begins full production and you'll have some flowers by Memorial Day. Keep a sharp eye out for pests, particularly snails and slugs.
JUNE-AUGUST	The heat will cause blooming to slow, but the plant will continue to grow. Lacecaps linger as the hortensias fade. Blooms can be harvested and hung to dry or left on the bush to dry naturally as "green flowers."
SEPTEMBER-OCTOBER	You'll see some copper-colored foliage as cool nights and shorter autumn days "lock" the pigments in the leaves.
NOVEMBER	Prime time to move your plant. Protected areas, along foundations, shady spots near corners will enhance the graceful beauty of this summer spectacle.
DECEMBER	Prune now. For a short, stocky plant, some folks like to prune their hydrangeas all the way back to the ground, removing all the brown parts. For a more graceful, arching shrub which will fill space more quickly in the spring, reduce the plant by no more than one-third. For a natural, pure hydrangea prune only selected stems for maintenance, and allow your plant to grow at will, expecting heights of six feet.

Ilex x attenuata 'Savannah'

Savannah holly

It's easy to see why Savannah hollies have become one of the most popular large shrubs or small trees in the coastal area. They are evergreen, yet show nice growth in the spring. They produce a sizeable crop of red berries in the winter, the foliage stays healthy even in the roughest weather and the tree has a rapid growth rate. It stands well on the corners of the foundation, looks great against the wall of a commercial building, and makes a very good streetside tree for the city. It has a natural cone shape which requires little, if any, pruning, and the Savannah is known for pest-free, trouble-free culture. For years this has been the "go to" holly of the coastal South, and it rarely disappoints.

But it does have a few drawbacks. The color is pale, not rich green, which causes some folks to overfeed it. It has been used so extensively that many people feel it is too common for exclusive areas. And the tree can become very chlorotic if the pH of the soil is not satisfactory.

There are other hybrids from the species that have captured the attention of homeowners and landscapers that may be as desirable. 'Hume's', 'East Palatka', and 'Foster's #2' have all scored significant sales. But, pound for pound, 'Savannah' still leads the pack as the choice holly from this group.

The ideal 'Savannah' will grow to eighteen feet with a spread of four feet. Streetside plantings and city culture will produce slightly less size.

MONTH-BY-MONTH GUIDE FOR SAVANNAH HOLLY

JANUARY	Though dormant, your holly will continue to show plenty of red berries.
FEBRUARY-MARCH	Dormancy, high winds and little rainfall may cause your plant to be weak and pale. This is completely normal and should not cause concern.
APRIL	The flowers are insignificant, though you can notice them along the branches. As soon as they fall, berries begin to form (though hard to detect), and the plant will show signs of growth.
MAY-JULY	Water your plant every other day. As the berries begin to form, water is the key to an excellent crop.
AUGUST	Prune now. You may cut away some of the fruiting, but the plant will have a chance to repair itself after pruning, and will quickly regain its shape. Fertilize with a single application of 5-10-10.
LABOR DAY	Replace the mulch and water your plant.
THANKSGIVING	Red berries have formed now, and your plant is producing lots of them for the holidays.
DECEMBER	Harvest a few branches, and after Christmas, feed your plant with a cup of superphosphate and half a cup of Epsom salts.

Ilex cornuta 'Burfordii'

Burford holly

Burford holly may be the most popular of the hollies grown in the coastal South, and for good reason. Tough, durable and with great appearance, this rotund beauty offers everything you want in a red-green holly. There is a dwarf variety for folks who prefer a smaller version. Otherwise, you can expect twenty feet of excellent growth from the hybrid shrub, though you can prune lower branches to encourage more terminal growth. The plant spreads quickly as it grows to a well-rounded maximum width of ten feet.

It is rumored that this hybrid was developed at a Wilmington nursery, though Burfords are found all over the South. The leaves are dark green, slightly convex, and have a single spine at the tip. They are mostly female plants and require a pollinator close by to make sure they produce plenty of the red berries for which they are famous. They require sunny locations in slightly acid soils and well drained humus in which to grow. They are best when featured in the garden as single plants, or at the foundation corners. Since they are most effective in the winter, place them where they can be seen and appreciated. A healthy, thick plant with lots of berries is hard to beat in the winter landscape, and wildlife, from rabbits to birds are a common sight.

Though pest-free, these plants quickly develop a sickly, yellow cast when undernourished, or when the the pH of the soil is too acid or too alkaline.

MONTH-BY-MONTH GUIDE FOR BURFORD HOLLY

JANUARY	Plenty of red berries persist on your dormant plant. Severe cold weather may curl the leaves and weaken the appearance of the plant, though your Burford is hardy.
FEBRUARY	Early arrivals of birds will feed heavily on the berries, often stripping the plant.
MARCH-APRIL	Your plant will break dormancy this period and bloom freely, though the flowers are often inconspicuous compared to other plants in the garden.
MAY-JUNE	Burfords show aggressive growth, often exceeding any planned size. Tip prune if needed.
JULY	Prune as needed. Your plant is drought-resistant.
AUGUST-SEPTEMBER	Fruits begin to appear as green berries. A yellow-leaved plant is a good sign it needs some attention. If it appears weak, apply half a cup of Epsom salts around the base, half a cup of 5-10-10 fertilizer and test the soil. Slightly acid soil is best. Amend the soil accordingly.
OCTOBER-NOVEMBER	Fruits turn from green to yellow and from yellow to orange. By Thanksgiving Day they are red.
DECEMBER	Dark green boughs and rich red berries are ideal for cutting during the holidays. Bring some Burford holly branches indoors for vases, swags and wreaths. The stems are heavy and thick, but worth the trouble it takes to work with them, especially since the colors are perfect for the season.

Ilex crenata

Japanese holly

'*Convexa*'   Typical of the species, this variety is female and has fruit. Plenty of dark green, glossy leaves.

'*Helleri*'   An ultra-small selection, perfect for low borders. Very small leaves. Tight, compact growth.

'*Compacta*'   Like '*Convexa*', but the leaf of this one is flatter while '*Convexa*' is cupped. This selection is easy to prune and shape. Nice globe shape.

'Green Luster'   Looser and more open than many *crenata* hybrids, the dark green shiny leaves will spread on slender branches up to eight feet. You can expect four feet of vertical growth.

Japanese hollies are widely used as landscape plants because they are very durable, pest-free, tolerant of many soil conditions, and readily available at excellent prices. They are often called "Box leaf holly," and are characterized by a global, shrubby growth habit, rounded, slightly serrated leaves and dense growth. Japanese hollies have been used extensively, and thus are not as popular in unique landscapes as they were ten years ago, but they are still excellent choices for carefree gardening because they are so easy to grow. The usual rules will do just fine for this one: well-drained soil, moderate to full sun and no more than an inch of water weekly.

Most varieties, except the low growers, will reach four or five feet tall with a mounded three-foot spread. The border plants will reach only a foot or so in height with a spread of eighteen inches.

MONTH-BY-MONTH GUIDE FOR JAPANESE HOLLY

JANUARY-FEBRUARY	Though dormant, this evergreen remains dark green through the remainder of the winter.
MARCH-APRIL	Warm days can encourage some new growth. Look for pale green leaves forming at the tips of the stems.
MAY-JUNE	New growth continues. Spider mites may be a problem. If so, treat them with a mild solution of soapy water and a teaspoon of household ammonia, dispensed though a standard pint spray bottle.
JULY	Some Japanese hollies develop a fungal disorder that causes sections of the plant to become sooty along the stems with yellow foliage which often dies. If this condition occurs, spray the entire plant with a commercial fungicide at the recommended dose, then again ten days later if needed. If the situation does not improve, prune away the affected parts.
AUGUST	Water is essential. Check the pH of the soil and amend accordingly. Prune at will.
SEPTEMBER-OCTOBER	Now is a good time to clean up around the base of the plant, replacing the mulch and opening the canopy above the bed. Late in October, you can relocate plants if needed.
NOVEMBER-DECEMBER	Your hollies are dormant.

Ilex x 'Nellie R. Stevens'

Nellie Stevens Holly

One of the best hollies for the coastal area, this hybrid offers some great characteristics: very fast growth up to several feet per year; rich, dark green foliage with a minimum number of spines per leaf; a heavy crop of dark red berries; and an excellent conical shape for the specimen tree in your landscape or as a windbreak or screen. This is the "go to" holly if you want classic holly looks. Expect fifteen to twenty-five feet of growth and a minimal spread with plenty of lush, dark green leaves.

Though tolerant of many soil conditions and exposures, the 'Nellies' seem to grow best in sunny locations, with rich soil and a liberal dose of fertilizer in the spring.

Check the soil pH yearly. Too acid a soil or too alkaline will cause your 'Nellie' to become pale and lethargic.

When others tell you to plant 'Savannah' or 'Burford' or another hybrid, take a break from their advice and consider a 'Nellie R.' It will quickly become the pride of your coastal landscape!

MONTH-BY-MONTH GUIDE FOR NELLIE R. STEVENS HOLLY

JANUARY	Red berries persist on your dormant holly.
FEBRUARY-MARCH	Birds and other wildlife have eaten the berries, and your plant shows rich green leaves.
APRIL-MAY	Test the soil, replace the mulch and get set for lots of growth.
JUNE-JULY	Pale green leaves erupt along the tips of the branches, and your 'Nellie' pushes a foot or more of new growth. Help it along with an application of 8-8-8- or 10-10-10 at the recommended rate. Now is a good time to amend the soil according to test results.
AUGUST-SEPTEMBER	You can prune some if you need to do so, but keep it to a minimum. Though you might not have noticed the flowers back in the spring, the result is a heavy crop of green berries appearing throughout the self-fruitful tree.
OCTOBER-NOVEMBER	Unless your plant is weak, you can expect a bumper crop year after year of dark red berries, most of which appear this period.
DECEMBER	Harvest a few branches for the holidays, but make shallow, balanced cuts. Don't take too much from any one section of the tree.

Illicium anisatum

Japanese anise tree

The anises are strong shrubs which provide gardeners with several species of ornamental plants. *I. anisatum* is a favorite of the coastal area because of its fragrant foliage (spicy, just like anise), tall, erect growth habit and ease in cultivation. The plant will gain twelve feet and spread only a few feet, so it's ideal for the corner of the foundation, in a natural setting or as a hedge. The leaves are well-spaced along the woody branches and stay green all year.

The plant has no pests and requires very little pruning, though you may want to trim the top branches every second year to control the height.

Japanese anise is easy to cultivate, but keep some things in mind. The foliage is pale green by nature. Don't overfertilize to encourage deeper green color; in fact, you should not feed the plant at all. A healthy soil base is the key to raising this plant, so partial sunshine locations with plenty of rich humus and annual applications of compost are essential, not commercial fertilizers. The plant will need moist soil, so never let it dry out. It will even tolerate wet soil, but never dry, sandy conditions.

Unlike other anises which have large, showy flowers, this species does not have a remarkable flower. But it makes a fine specimen because of its foliage, and will provide an uncommon appearance in your coastal garden.

MONTH-BY-MONTH GUIDE FOR JAPANESE ANISE TREE

JANUARY-FEBRUARY	The plant is dormant, but evergreen.
MARCH	Water the plant as soon as danger of frost is over and apply several gallons of compost around the base of the plant. Replace the mulch with fresh, dry material.
APRIL-MAY	You'll notice some new growth along the branches and in the terminals of the stems. Insignificant white flowers also appear. Your plant should be watered every other day or so. Keep the water consistent and even.
JUNE-AUGUST	Prune unwanted growth during the summer. As you cultivate around the plant, be careful not to disturb the roots or scatter lawn fertilizers around the base. As you work around the plant you'll notice the strong, spicy aroma from the leaves.
SEPTEMBER-OCTOBER	Replace the mulch and test the soil. Slightly acid pH is best. Amend accordingly.
NOVEMBER-DECEMBER	Some yellow foliage may appear as the days get shorter. Unlike some other evergreens which make good holiday decorations, the foliage from this plant will not last long after cutting.

Juniperus conferta 'Blue Pacific'

Shore juniper

This variety of shore juniper is very popular, so much so that we see it used all over the surrounding landscape, from dune and and berm erosion control to container gardens and rock-bordered gardens. It grows quickly and can ramble over low walls, covering bulkheads and slopes in a very short time. Owners of commercial sites love it for its low maintenance and quick coverage. Homeowners use it for massed beds and for covering bare ground.

Some say it is overused, and that we see too much of it. But the utility of it may surpass its beauty. This is the workhorse of the junipers. Growing to eighteen inches tall and spreading twice that amount in two growing seasons, it starts the spring with a quick green-up of light, feathery spikes, then "hardens" to a rich carpet of blue-green foliage.

It's common, but it's pest-free, tolerates a wide range of soils and provides excellent ground coverage. It does not tolerate shade very well, and the mistake many people make in initial planting is placing it too thinly. Install this wonderful ground cover on twelve inch centers and watch it grow all over the bed for many years to come.

A fungal blight may kill the tips of the branches, turning your juniper from green to brown. If this happens a soil drench of a basic garden fungicide will probably restore health and vigor. Shore juniper is ideal for coastal plantings where salt tolerance is needed.

MONTH-BY-MONTH GUIDE FOR SHORE JUNIPER

JANUARY-FEBRUARY	The dormant plant stays steely-green, even in the harshest weather.
MARCH-APRIL	Some leaf tip action may become noticeable. Look for tight green buds at the terminals.
MAY-JUNE	Growth along the branches erupts now as your shore juniper expands rapidly. You will notice some upward growth as well as expansion growth. This is quite normal, and the height of the plant should be of no concern as it will "lay down" later.
JULY-AUGUST	Brown leaf tips indicate a fungal blight.Using a gallon bucket, mix a full dose of a basic garden fungicide at the recommended rate and pour the mixture into the soil around the base of the plant. Control is immediate and effective. Shear as needed.
SEPTEMBER-OCTOBER	New growth has turned color now, and the foliage is a rich blue-green shade. Dormancy approaches.
NOVEMBER-DECEMBER	Bring a few selected stems inside for long-lasting holiday decorations.

Juniperus davurica 'Expansa'

Parson's juniper

If it's juniper you want, here's the one to grow in the coastal garden, especially if you want a prostrate shrub with a low growth habit. With a maximum height of eighteen inches and a spread of at least that much in most directions, it will form a dense ground cover. Rich, blue-green foliage with scale-like leaves forms a mass that can provide excellent ground coverage. '*Variegata*' has the same growth habit and foliage, but is tinted with creamy-yellow leaf tips.

Parson's is an ideal, carefree plant. A conifer, it bears small cones which are mildly aromatic, and it takes the heat of the coastal garden. Plant it in full sun. It is perfect for slopes, massed beds, grouped in enclosed gardens or as a specimen in your flower garden.

Ordinary soil is best, slightly acid in pH, and you needn't worry about fertilizers or pest controls. Forget pruning too, and enjoy this plant with its blue color cast. It's the one landscape addition that you'll enjoy for years without having to maintain it! Parson's grows well in salty, beach exposures, provided that the soil base contains enough humus to support strong growth.

MONTH-BY-MONTH GUIDE FOR PARSON'S JUNIPER

JANUARY	The dormant plant may have a slight purple tint during extremely cold periods.
FEBRUARY-MARCH	Replace old mulch, and rake beneath the plant for appearances only.
APRIL-JUNE	New growth pushes from all parts of the plant, appears as light, pale green foliage, then turns a steely-blue color.
JULY-SEPTEMBER	If whole sections of the plant die after turning brown and you notice a lot of "needle" loss, be suspicious of fungal disorders. Prune away dead material and drench the soil around the base of the plant with a fungicide mixed with a gallon of water, following the label directions carefully.
OCTOBER-NOVEMBER	When other plants lose vitality as dormancy approaches, your Parson's juniper will still be healthy and vigorous.
DECEMBER	Dormancy sets in, all other garden plants fade, but your Parson's becomes more obvious in the landscape with its crisp blue-green foliage.

Kerria japonica

Japanese kerria

It's probably best to shop for this plant in the spring when it blooms so that you can see the wonderful color and arching growth habit that make it so desirable in the coastal garden. The bright orange-yellow flowers are a great addition to the usual pink, red and peach colors of the spring landscape, and since the flowers form along the long graceful branches of dark green foliage, kerria can be planted with azaleas and other shrubbier plants easily. The genus contains only one species, and there are only a few cultivated varieties, so a request for Japanese kerria may yield a plant that has more yellow than orange flowers. Or you may get a variety that has brilliant, double, orange blossoms. In any case, you will be surprised at the ease in growing and maintenance-free cultivation. Plant in well-drained soil, and your kerria will bloom in partial shade, though shade causes longer branches and less flowering than if your plant gets a full five hours of diffused sunlight every day. Prune only if needed, and remember that kerria will grow to eight feet with an arching habit, so install your plant with these things in mind.

MONTH-BY-MONTH GUIDE FOR KERRIA

JANUARY	Kerria is semi-deciduous, so your dormant plant may have a few small leaves. Look for dark green stems as a sign of good dormant health. It's a good time to repair the mulch and amend the flower bed.
FEBRUARY-MARCH	Balmy days will cause the plant to sprout some leaves. Kerria foliates about the same time that it flowers.
APRIL	Flower buds suddenly appear as warm days approach. Flowering along the arches comes quickly and lasts for several weeks.
MAY	Prune now if you need to shape your plant. Tip pruning and light shearing will cause more branching. Next year's flowers are borne on this season's growth.
JUNE-AUGUST	Water is essential. Lacebugs may be a slight problem and can be treated with a basic insecticide like pyrethrins or DE. Get a soil test. Kerria grows best in slightly acidic soil. Amend according to the test and fertilize with a light dose of 6-6-12 before August fifteenth. Some flowering continues.
SEPTEMBER-OCTOBER	Some flowering takes place this period. Don't be surprised to see plenty of flowers before your kerria slips into dormancy. A dose of superphosphate will help blooming next season.
NOVEMBER	Replace the mulch and clean up around the base of the plant.
DECEMBER	Leaves lose some color and turn yellow. Most will fall away now as your kerria drops into the dormant cycle.

Lagerstroemia indica

Crape myrtle

There are many cultivars in this species, all of which will perform well in the coastal area. The new National Arboretum hybrids, developed at the National Arboretum in Washington, D.C., have excellent flowers, thick foliage and superb fall color. Though somewhat difficult to find in local nurseries, they are worth the effort in tracking down.

One of the most famous plants in the Southern landscape, these small trees and shrubs will bloom all summer with a vigorous growth habit. They can be pruned hard every season, or allowed to grow at will, depending on your landscape requirements. Plant your crape myrtle in a sunny location for good blooming in well-drained, slightly acid soil. Pay close attention to the pruning dates in the guide, and avoid spreading lawn grass fertilizers within three feet of the base of your tree. Watch for Japanese beetles in the summer, and treat them with pyrethrins or rotenone. Powdery mildew often attacks the new leaves in spring and, though rarely a major problem, this fungus can make the shrub unsightly. Mild cases can be treated with a solution of baking soda and water at the rate of a quarter cup of baking soda per gallon of water. Severe cases may require synthetic fungicides. Good air circulation and sunlight are the keys to excellent blooming and will help create the large, colorful, crape-like flowers this tree is noted for. Also called "Indian Lilacs" by old-timers, *Lagerstroemia indica* is a Southern classic and a mainstay of the Carolina coastal garden.

The old standbys, like 'Carolina Beauty' and 'Country Red' are tall growers and will exceed twenty-five feet if left unpruned. The plants will spread over ten feet if left unpruned. Some cultivars grow slightly less in size. It is always best to purchase your plant while it is in bloom since the color choices are many, and you will perhaps like to select one that best suits a particular color scheme. Crape myrtles bloom on current season's growth.

MONTH-BY-MONTH GUIDE FOR CRAPE MYRTLE

JANUARY-FEBRUARY	Your tree or shrub is dormant.
MARCH-APRIL	Prepare for spring break. Avoid wounding the tree with your line-trimmer or power tools. Keep the base of the tree raked and clean.
MAY 20TH	Fertilize today with half a cup of 6-6-12 or 5-10-10 fertilizer, one-quarter cup of magnesium sulfate and one-fourth cup of superphosphate around the drip line and walk it into the soil with your golf spikes.
JULY 15th	Fertilize today with one-quarter cup of 6-6-12.
AUGUST-SEPTEMBER	Treat pests as they appear. When blooming stops on any branch lightly prune to prolong blossoming.
NOVEMBER 27th	Prune this week. As soon as the plant changes color and drops leaves prune away unwanted wood, twisted stems and damaged limbs. Reduce as much as you want, but at least by one-third.
DECEMBER	This is the month for good sanitation. Rake and mow around the base, but be careful not to wound the trunk.

Ligustrum lucidum

Glossy Privet

The species contains a few cultivated varieties, but you'll do just fine here in the coastal area with the species plant. In fact, when you ask the nurseryman for glossy privet, he might well know it as Chinese privet, and he may have only one type in stock. The privet family is large and contains many familiar plants. Over the years, the genus has become confused, even to plant professionals. But once you have agreed you are purchasing glossy privet, you are purchasing a plant with which you will never have a cultural problem. Whether you hedge it, box it, let it go in the mixed bed, use it as a screen for outbuildings or as a foundation plant, this evergreen, dense shrub will not disappoint you.Strong, thick and aggressive, glossy privet is maintenance-free, and your biggest chore may be pruning it to the size you prefer. When grown in the sun, the plant has an abundance of creamy-white, highly fragrant flowers in early spring, followed by several cycles of growth. If you choose partial shade, you'll have fewer flowers, but plenty of green growth. Pruning, if any, is done anytime during the year, and your glossy privet will need little or no fertilizer.

Expect your plant to reach a height of ten feet with a spread of four feet.

MONTH-BY-MONTH GUIDE FOR GLOSSY PRIVET

JANUARY	Though dormant, your plant will display bright, dark green foliage.
FEBRUARY	In severe weather, see some signs of cold damage, which may be copper-colored foliage or in severe cases, blackened leaf margins.
MARCH	In balmy weather, some growth is not unusual.
APRIL-MAY	Flowering takes place this period and new growth is obvious. As soon as it hardens prune the desired amount of foliage away from the top and sides of the plant.
JUNE-AUGUST	Robust plants grow freely, but the summer heat may trigger a brief dormant period in late summer. Chewed leaf margins indicate caterpillars which can be treated with Dipel. Shot holes in the leaves indicate flea beetles which can be treated with pyrethrins. Pale foliage may indicate a problem with soil pH.
SEPTEMBER	A good month to fertilize, if need be. Try a balanced formula like 8-8-8.
OCTOBER-DECEMBER	Prepare for winter by replacing the mulch. Light pruning and transplanting or moving can be done now.

Liriodendron tulipifera

Tulip poplar

Poplars are one of the most dynamic and magnificent shade trees of the coastal area of the Carolinas. They are fast growers and very vigorous, and have all the advantages of traditional shade trees, being pest-free and requiring very little care. Mature trees have deeply furrowed bark, a light colored trunk, straight-up growth habit and a high canopy of maple-like foliage that becomes a brilliant yellow in the fall. They will easily reach 120 feet and can grow as much as six feet in a single season. The wood is tough and durable and resists storm damage as well as any native tree because the root system is deep and wide.

The tree is called tulip poplar because of its orange and yellow flowers in the early spring. These flowers resemble tulips in structure and are borne throughout the tree before foliage appears. The leaves are pale green and are among the first to appear in the spring. Grow this tree as a specimen shade tree in an isolated location, allow it to grow at will, and do not prune it. Slightly acid soil is best, and moist conditions suit it perfectly. As the tree grows, make sure it has all the water it needs. Younger trees need to be protected from aphids.

MONTH-BY-MONTH GUIDE FOR TULIP POPLAR

JANUARY-FEBRUARY	The dormant tree should be protected in early years from wind damage and freezing soil.
MARCH-APRIL	Poplars are among the first trees to break dormancy. Look for yellow and orange tulip-like flowers to appear along the branches. These are obvious in young trees, not so much in older ones. Water is essential. If the season is dry, make sure the tree has one inch of water every five days. Encourage the root system to expand by keeping the base clear of other ornamentals.
MAY	The tree is fully foliated now as summer approaches. Plenty of maple-like leaves cover the canopy. If you notice aphids in young trees, treat several times with pyrethrins, or use a steady stream of soapy water as needed.
JUNE -AUGUST	Water is crucial. Never let the tree wilt or dry out. Use a basic organic mulch around the base. Check the soil pH and amend it to 5.5 or 6.
SEPTEMBER	Poplars change color rapidly, and are among the first trees to drop their leaves. The fall color is yellow, and old flower pods are obvious as the leaves fall.
OCTOBER-NOVEMBER	Most leaves are gone now as the tree becomes dormant.
DECEMBER	You should not need to prune the tree, but storm damaged limbs can be removed if you notice them. Change the mulch.

Loropetalum chinense

Loropetalum

Another Asian plant, this wonderful ornamental has all the characteristics so desirable for the coastal garden. David Barkley, urban horticulturist for the North Carolina Extension Service, calls this plant "the hottest landscape plant to come on the market in twenty-five years," and it's easy to see why. Its ease of cultivation, well-rounded shape and fragrant, creamy-white flowers in late winter or early spring make it ideal for coastal gardens. Loropetalum grows quickly to become a casual, graceful foundation plant or featured landscape specimen. It resembles privet, but doesn't have the weedy, common look associated with that old Southern standby.

Loropetalum grows best in well-drained, slightly acid soil, will tolerate a fair amount of shade and can grow in open sunshine. You can prune it at will, but it's best left alone so you can enjoy all the texture, mounded growth habit and flowering of this magnificent shrub. Plant it wisely, because it will achieve twelve feet of growth and a spread of nine feet at maturity.

It's hard to find and slightly expensive, so plan ahead and order in advance, but it's worth the wait and the cost. Some new cultivars have pink flowers and variegated foliage, and a recent creation has nice, plum-colored leaves.

122

MONTH- BY- MONTH GUIDE FOR LOROPETALUM

JANUARY	Some leaf loss is apparent, but for the most part, the dormant plant is idle.
FEBRUARY-MARCH	Flower buds appear along the branches, and you might notice some flowering late in March. Whole branches may burst into bloom on a warm March day, surprising you with the fragrance. New leaf growth is obvious.
APRIL	Flowering continues or slows, depending on the weather. New growth takes place now as the winter days wane and spring arrives.
MAY	Prune any time now, but remember that boxing and shearing this ornamental will destroy the wonderful, casual growth habit. You might consider moving it later in the fall rather than pruning it too severely.
JUNE-AUGUST	Growth continues at a steady rate, though hot, humid days in late summer don't produce much activity.
LABOR DAY	Test the soil. You need slightly acidic, rich, well-drained material. Do you need to change the basic growing conditions?
OCTOBER	Amend the soil according to the test.
THANKSGIVING	Transplant or move the plant today if you wish.
DECEMBER	Falling leaves are an indication your loropetalum is going to sleep for the winter.

Magnolia grandiflora

Southern magnolia, Bull bay

Alice B. Russell

In the moist soils of the Southeast coastal area, you'll find this magnificent native evergreen. The thick, dark green leaves often have a coarse, bronze-colored bark and the tree will reach a full eighty feet at maturity. The conical shape with branches that often droop to the ground make this shade tree one of the most desirable in any large landscape.

The magnolia is the oldest of the angiosperms (trees that produce flowers as the chief means of pollination, as opposed to gymnosperms which depend on wind-driven pollination for reproduction). The flowers are very large and fragrant, which makes them so attractive in the Southern landscape.

This beautiful native shade tree will dominate a site. It loses leaves several times during the year, once in the spring as it pushes new foliage, and again in the fall. This shedding is a disadvantage for some homeowners because the tough, slippery leaves are hard to rake. But despite this drawback, a magnolia is a wonderful addition to any large garden, and you should allow this elegant tree to grow without pruning.

Magnolias will grow in any average soil, but they will not tolerate compacted conditions, "wet feet," or severe drought. Many of the branches will grow close to the ground, so don't plant ornamental shrubbery around the base. Open sites are best because sunshine increases blooming.

The "cones" of magnolias are cylindrical fruits which bear bright red seeds. Birds will feed on them, but many fall to the ground where they germinate, creating lots of new seedlings. If you harvest a few of the fruits before they dry on the tree, you can use them in holiday decorations.

Magnolia foliage can be preserved easily by placing a few short branches in a vase of half-water and half-glycerine. Leave the branches in the solution for six weeks, replenishing the glycerine-water mixture as needed. The foliage will change color to a deep brown or tan, but will keep its supple nature. You can do this anytime during the year except when the foliage is tender.

MONTH-BY-MONTH GUIDE FOR MAGNOLIA

JANUARY-MARCH	The tree is dormant but remains vibrant in the winter landscape.
APRIL	Some new stem growth appears in the form of furry, brown elongated sprouts in the axils of branches. Older leaves may turn yellow and fall from the tree.
MAY	Flowers appear, and leaves fall to the ground.
JUNE	This is the main season for blooming. Eight-inch flowers with six or more petals open slowly along the branches, some with pronounced red pistils. The flowers are highly fragrant and last for several days before turning brown and dropping. The blooms bruise easily when harvested.
JULY-AUGUST	Blooming slows during the heat of the summer.
SEPTEMBER-OCTOBER	It's not uncommon to see a few flowers along the branches, but the main growth of the tree takes place in the terminals of the branches as new leaves "harden." Later in the fall, some leaves drop from the tree. Because the leaves are thick, leathery and slippery, they are hard to collect. Mature fruits appear in the form of spiny "cones." These bear bright red, pulpy seeds which fall to the ground as the cones dry and split.
NOVEMBER-DECEMBER	Dormancy arrives, and the tree is one of the few in the landscape that remains green. Cut a few branches for holiday decorations and display them along mantels or in tall vases.

Magnolia x soulangeana (soulangiana)

Saucer magnolia

'Alba Superba'   Medium-sized white flowers with a purple shade are highly fragrant and bloom early.

'Rustica Rubra'   Often grown in the South, this deep purple flower is striking against a blue spring sky.

'Brozonii'   A frequently planted cultivar, this M. *x soulangeana* becomes a large tree with large purple-white flowers, very popular as a featured landscape tree. It has an upright growth habit, not spreading.

What a family these magnolias are! So familiar to us in the South, the large M. *grandiflora* (Bull bay) leads the pack with the familiar summer blossoms and deep, rich foliage. But an equally impressive tree is this first cousin, the hybrid M. *x soulangeana* , and all of its cultivated varieties, a few of which are listed. One of the first trees to flower in the spring, M. *x soulangeana* shows us its saucer-shaped blooms long before the pale green foliage that follows. In fact, the tree blooms so early, it is often clipped by late winter blasts which freeze the flowers. Even so, it is worth planting, because there are perhaps only a few other flowering spring trees that rival this beauty. A checklist of advantages shows you why: large, early flowers that are highly fragrant, often lasting ten days or more; lush, green foliage offering summer shade, wildlife protection and breezy aesthetics; full canopy that stays green and stays up a long time; rich, golden fall color and rapid leaf loss which makes for one-time raking; and a stark winter skyline of branches and twigs which are always capped by flower buds swelling slowly as spring approaches. Whichever cultivar you select, you'll be choosing a tree that will quickly become a favorite. Only follow the advice of hundreds of experienced growers: let this tree stand alone, unpruned, and feature it in a sunny, breezy spot that you can see from lots of windows. If you have space for only one specimen tree, if your soil is well-drained, slightly acid and rich in humus, if you like carefree gardening, and if you'd like to turn the heads of your neighbors, then you should plant this wonderful coastal Carolina classic! (Note: Folks often call this the "tulip tree." That is a mistake, of course, but the name persists. To make sure you are planting the actual saucer magnolia, ask for it by its botanical name.)

Some varieties of this tree spread out rather than grow tall, but most will reach a height of twenty feet and a width of fifteen feet or slightly more.

MONTH-BY-MONTH GUIDE FOR SAUCER MAGNOLIA

JANUARY	Your tree is showing some signs of spring break.
FEBRUARY	A mild, springlike day may cause a flower or two to break. Late in the month the entire tree could burst into bloom.
MARCH	If it hasn't done so already, the whole tree will flower rapidly at any time. Pick up the spent blossoms and and prune now if need be.
APRIL	Foliage will develop rapidly now as the tree rests awhile. Leave it alone for the rest of the spring and summer .
MAY-JULY	Some slight leaf loss is okay, and late in the summer apply a cup or so of superphosphate around the drip line. Avoid fertilizers, especially those that you are using on the lawn grass.
SEPTEMBER-NOVEMBER	Caterpillars may nibble some leaves, but birds will enjoy the canopy. So, avoid spraying the tree unless you see a major problem. Rake up the fall leaves quickly and keep the grass trimmed beneath the tree.
DECEMBER	Total leaf loss takes place as dormancy arrives.

Malus floribunda

Japanese flowering crabapple

This deciduous ornamental tree is one of the most popular in the area. A height of twenty-five feet and a spread of thirty feet or more make it ideal for coastal gardens and it is often featured in open landscapes, commercial sites and residential settings where folks have enough room to grow this beautiful shade tree.

It has plenty of cousins, like the 'Callaway' crabapple and M. *sargentii*, a tree which we discuss in this book. But this species is particularly nice for the Carolina coastal garden because of its early spring flowers, maroon-colored foliage in spring and early summer and the fruit, which attracts birds in the fall.

It has a few pests and requires some pruning every other year, but the tree can be a valuable part of your landscape, so it's worth the trouble. Bag worms build nests in the late summer. Eliminate them by spraying the tree with a basic fruit tree spray, or simply knock the webs out of the branches with a reach pole. A fungal blight might attack the leaves. This can be controlled with the fruit tree spray in early years, but may be more complicated to control as the tree matures. The disease is unsightly, but rarely harms the overall health. M. *floribunda* is an aggressive grower which generates a lot of branches. As they grow, they may criss-cross in your line of vision, so to keep the appearance 'clean', you will need to remove unwanted branches every other year.

This is a delightful tree. From early spring when the deep pink flower buds first appear, to late fall when the small crabapples attract scores of birds, you'll be proud to have it in your collection of ornamentals.

MONTH-BY-MONTH GUIDE FOR JAPANESE FLOWERING CRABAPPLE

JANUARY-FEBRUARY	The tree is dormant. Rake beneath it to collect old leaves and debris.
MARCH	Water the tree. Early in the month, spray the trunk and bare branches with horticultural oil. Late in the month, flower buds will swell, and a few may pop open on a warm day.
APRIL	The tree will bloom early in the month. The buds are deep pink or maroon, but open as pale pink, almost white flowers with five petals and pronounced stamens. The flowers will linger for a week or more, followed by strong leafing. The new leaves are maroon at first, but will change to green during the growing season.
MAY	Rake beneath the tree. As you begin fertilizing other plants and the lawn around the tree, remember not to overfeed your crabapple.
JUNE-AUGUST	A muggy summer may cause some fungal blight. In older trees this will be hard to control, but in younger trees, you can treat the condition with a fruit tree spray. It's best not to treat the condition unless you have a severe problem. As summer wanes, you might notice some bag worms. The fruit tree spray, or Dipel will control them, or you can knock the webs down with a reach pole. Some leaf loss late in the summer is normal. The small crabapples are obvious in the branches.
SEPTEMBER-NOVEMBER	Leaf loss takes place as the days get shorter. The fall color is not remarkable. As soon as all leaves are down, observe the tree's branches. Do you need to prune some crossing limbs? Birds will take over the tree to eat the fruit.
DECEMBER	If you haven't pruned, do so now. Some light raking and good garden sanitation is an easy task on a winter day.

Malus sargentii

Sargent crabapple

This is the one crabapple that offers a challenge. From the purchase of the tree to maintaining it, homeowners need to pay attention to the process.

Unfortunately, you'll have to know a little about this "crab-tree" before you purchase it. You'll want to buy grafted stock, so ask your nurseryman to make sure your tree was not grown from seed. You'll avoid a Sargent that grows more like a shrub. Grafted stock will not get above fourteen feet or so but can often spread that much, so choose its location wisely. It makes an excellent specimen, can be grouped or placed along a stream bank or hillside, but open areas with well-drained soil and plenty of sunshine are ideal. The fruits, which can form all summer, are the choice food for many birds, so pick a spot that encourages wildlife.

The cultivation of this species is detailed because the better care you give it, the more you'll avoid the "ups and downs" of this crabapple. If left unattended, it will produce an excellent show of flowers in alternate years only, and may develop one or more of the common apple diseases and pests—like apple-cedar rust, blight and mildew. A certified killer is wet soil, and if you plant this tree close to junipers, you'll have fungal problems. It blooms later than most spring-flowering trees, and so can be affected by by late frosts. To ensure that you have an actual "tree" rather than a "shrub" you should prune some of the lower branches in the first year or two.

But despite all that is required, the Sargent crabapple can be a great addition to your garden. The buds form late, beginning as tight, red or pink balls, but open to pure white fragrant flowers which last a week or more. It's not a popular tree, so you won't be growing something that you see on every corner. The fruits are dark red and glossy and attract scores of birds in the fall, and the foliage is as close to an apple's foliage as any species comes. And when everyone else's flowering fruit trees have long since dropped their petals, your Sargent crabapple will be in full flower!

It's worth the effort, and I believe in the value of this one so much that it was my only choice for a flowering fruit tree for my family's cemetery lot.

MONTH-BY-MONTH GUIDE FOR SARGENT CRABAPPLE

JANUARY	Prune away any damaged or broken limbs from your dormant tree and spray it completely with a dormant horticultural oil late in the month.
FEBRUARY-MARCH	Water is crucial, but do not let your tree stand in "wet feet." Replace the mulch, have the soil tested and protect the tree from late freezes.
APRIL	Flower buds may become obvious.
MAY	The tree will bloom any time as the days get warmer.
JUNE-AUGUST	Keep a watchful eye for diseases. A basic fruit tree spray is all that's needed, but you may have to be persistent with several applications.
SEPTEMBER 20TH	Replace the mulch. Any final pruning can be done now, especially if there is damaged or diseased material.
OCTOBER	Feed the tree with a cup of Sul-Po-Mag applied around the drip line and watered in.
NOVEMBER-DECEMBER	Normal maintenance and raking now as dormancy sets in.

Myrica cerifera

Wax myrtle, Bayberry

There have been a few attempts at developing cultivated varieties of this famous Southern shrub, but the species plant is just fine for your coastal Carolina garden. It tolerates salt spray, will grow in most soil types and can survive just about anything that nature throws its way. Bayberry is the famous scent of Williamsburg candles, made from reducing and refining the blue berries in the fall. The foliage, brought inside for Christmas, is wonderfully fragrant, and can be used for scenting cedar chests and wardrobes. The colonists traded wax myrtle as a commodity, and in our search for things that remind us of colonial America, Southern wax myrtle is at the top of the list. Useful as a hedge, screen or native group planting, wax myrtle can hide unsightly buildings, cover banks or ridges or can even be featured as a remarkable specimen. Easy to grow, rapid in development and inexpensive to purchase, this native should be a part of every home landscape. The month-by-month guide illustrates the ease with which you can grow this plant, and it is perhaps the simplest of our indigenous plants to cultivate. Bayberry reaches eighteen feet in height and eight to ten feet in width.

MONTH-BY-MONTH GUIDE FOR WAX MYRTLE

JANUARY	Your plant is dormant. Small leaves which curl during the winter's coldest periods are normal signs of the plant's dormancy.
FEBRUARY-MARCH	This is a good time to prune, though your wax myrtle will push new growth several times during the growing season, and can be tip-pruned then.
APRIL	The plant is very aromatic, and the new growth which appears this month will be lightly scented.
MAY-AUGUST	Keep your plant well watered, but do not allow it to stand in water-logged soil. Small, insignificant flowers along the branch ends and tips will produce the small bluish-gray beads of fruit later in the season.
SEPTEMBER-OCTOBER	Do not prune or shear plants during this period because you may distort the shape of the plant for the remainder of the season. Newly pruned plants will produce some pale green growth which may be killed in an early frost or freeze.
NOVEMBER-DECEMBER	Holidays are excellent times to enjoy some branches of Bayberry indoors. Cut them long and deep, and aim for some that have the berries along the stems. Crushing the foliage will increase the fragrance.

Nandina domestica

Nandina, Heavenly bamboo

'Firepower'   A dwarfed plant with brilliant red-orange variegated foliage, used in low borders and massed groups. Though somewhat garish, this little plant will produce lots of bamboo-like foliage.

'Nana Purpurea'   No variegation with this dwarf, but plenty of foliage that turns plum-colored and red in the fall. Border material, and a low grower.

'Harbour Dwarf'   Another low grower, no taller than several feet. This one has the ability to change color more rapidly in the fall and shows lots of fruit around Thanksgiving.

The species plant, not the hybrid dwarf, is an old-fashioned plant that has been cultivated in the South for years. This Asian native is bamboo-like with long, graceful leaves containing lots of lance-shaped leaflets, most of which remain on the plant after turning color from green to deep maroon in the fall. The plant will flower in the spring with long spikes of fragrant white flowers which mature into grape-like clusters of rich red berries which last all winter. This is a durable plant, often thriving despite years of neglect.

The species plant matures at a height of ten feet with a width of five feet. It prefers moist, rich soil and good winter protection, and is usually left unpruned, though every third year or so, it helps to remove older canes by cutting them all the way back to the ground in early spring. Go for the canes in the center of the plant so you'll open up the plant and increase its natural arching gracefulness.

Plant the species plant at the corners of the foundation, in corners of walls and buildings, or featured in a natural setting. The newer, low-growing hybrids are best used in massed plantings, in the angles of curbing, or as buffers for garden accessories such as lights or sprinkler heads.

Nandina is easy to come by, inexpensive and not all that common. You'll be pleased with the seasonal advantage of red berries and wonderful fall foliage, both of which last a long time.

MONTH-BY-MONTH GUIDE FOR NANDINA

JANUARY	Red berries persist during this dormant period. The plant won't lose any foliage, but the leaves have turned some color, either bright red, purple or plum-colored.
FEBRUARY-MARCH	Nothing happens with your nandina, but some of the berries may drop or get lost to wildlife.
APRIL	Signs of growth take place, and late this month you may notice some flowering taking place. Leaves come to life, and you'll see more green foliage than the plum colors of winter.
MAY	Flowering takes place. Notice long panicles of white spikes, some fragrance and plenty of new growth. As soon as flowering stops, prune central canes all the way down to the ground. Don't shear the plant because you will create an odd-looking umbrella type appearance that destroys the elegance of the arching growth habit. A weak plant is rare but, if you feel the need, push your nandina along with a light dose of 8-8-8.
JUNE-AUGUST	No need to pay any attention to your nandina. It'll be just fine in the garden with no care.
LABOR DAY	Fruit is forming now. Look for green berries. You'll enhance fruiting and flowering for next season by applying a light dose of superphosphate around the base of the plant and working it into the soil.
OCTOBER-THANKSGIVING	Red berries are obvious now, and the foliage begins to turn color. Bring some of the berries indoors for a holiday decoration.
DECEMBER	Full color change takes place, and when all else is stark in the winter garden, nandina shows seasonal appeal. The dwarfed varieties have lots of foliage and you'll have plenty of red berries for the holidays.

Nerium Oleander

Oleander

! ALL PARTS OF THE PLANT ARE POISONOUS !

Oleander is the only species in this small genus of evergreen shrubs which are grown for their striking summertime flowers. Though they are frost tender and most oleanders are affected by winter freezes, they are worth growing because of their exceptional bloom and growth habit. Left alone to grow at will, they become large graceful shrubs with long branches which are perfect for capturing a summer breeze. If they are pruned, they can be held to compact sizes that develop into thicker, more rounded shrubs, though these plants tend to bloom less than the oleanders which are allowed to stretch. Pruning is done in the dormant season, and the plant will bloom in early to mid-summer, then again in the fall. Since the Carolina coastal area is at the northernmost edge of the growing region for oleanders, almost every season can be dangerous. Foliage which has been desiccated by winter winds usually falls away after turning brown, black and brittle. So, tip pruning may create a gangly plant that has an odd shape at the top and bare stems at the bottom. If your oleander has been severely "burned" by the winter, you may as well prune it back to twelve inches, sacrifice some flowering, and allow it to grow back over several seasons. If, however, damage is light, then you should prune no more than a third of the plant. An alternative pruning method is to select interior canes which cause crowded growth and to prune them each season. Your plant will become thinner but taller.

Old oleanders that have survived many seasons finish growing at twelve feet or so. They spread over three feet, but the growth habit is more tall than wide. It is rare, however, to have an oleander survive without some pruning which limits the maximum height and width. Choose a sunny spot that is well-drained and rich in soil content. Protected oleanders grow well along the coast and can tolerate some salt spray.

MONTH-BY-MONTH GUIDE FOR OLEANDER

JANUARY	Your plant is dormant though some foliage remains green and healthy.
FEBRUARY-MARCH	Ensure protection from foul weather and in late February by applying superphosphate around the base of the plant at the rate of one-fourth cup per three feet of plant height. Prune now.
APRIL	Water is essential as your plant pushes new growth. No more pruning. Fertilize around Easter with a cup of 6-6-12 or 5-10-10.
MAY-JUNE	Watch as your oleander grows and develops flower buds. A flower or two is not uncommon.
JULY-SEPTEMBER	This is the period when your plant will reach its peak. Pests will be few, and flowers will be plenty! Water is essential, and if your plant slacks a little it will rebound in slightly cooler weather. Apply another dose of superphosphate.
OCTOBER-NOVEMBER	Growth slows now as the days get shorter, but some flowering may continue.
DECEMBER	Leaf color turns from green to gray as your plant becomes dormant. Protect it from bad weather.

Nyssa sylvatica

Black gum, Tupelo

Of the tall shade trees that are native to the coastal Carolinas, few have the ease in growing, appeal and strength of the tupelo. Though it grows throughout the South, especially in the Gulf Coast areas, it has become one of the prized parts of cultivated landscapes here in our area. As its native sites are destroyed for development, many builders replant black gums for their quick growth and landscape versatility. Straight trunks have furrowed bark, short limbs with plenty of foliage, berry-like fruits which feed wildlife and wonderful fall color. The leaves are among the first to change color in the fall, from deep-green to rich, burgundy-red. They are pest-free and require little care. Grow your tupelo in moist, even wet soil, either shade or open sunshine, and avoid fertilizers. Do not prune it.

A favorite nesting tree for birds, small animals and a perch for hawks, the black gum will exceed eighty feet with a mass of short branches and heavy foliage that extend the length of the trunk.

MONTH-BY-MONTH GUIDE FOR TUPELO

JANUARY-FEBRUARY	Your tree is dormant, and the stark branches are bare.
MARCH-APRIL	One of the first trees to show foliage in the spring, the tupelo shows some new leaves any time during this period along with some insignificant flowers which drop catkins around the base.
MAY-JUNE	Keep young trees well-watered. Keep the lawn grass fertilizers away from the tree.
JULY-SEPTEMBER	Late in the period, you;'ll notice some black fruits falling from the tree. This fruit is very valuable as part of the mast.
OCTOBER-NOVEMBER	Older limbs which have died can be pruned away before all foliage falls. The tree will change color, becoming one of the most brilliant in the landscape.
DECEMBER	The dormant tree is bare.

Osmanthus fortunei

Fortune's osmanthus

Of all the osmanthus species, this one is perhaps the most durable for coastal landscapes. Besides durability, it offers lots of other advantages. You can allow it to grow as part of featured plantings at the corners of the foundation so it reaches its full height of twelve feet, or you can top it from time to time and allow it to spread out. It forms an excellent hedge, or it makes a good addition to a mixed ornamental bed.

Don't confuse this species with the other types of osmanthus, like holly leaf osmanthus and fragrant osmanthus, sometimes called fragrant olive. Fortune's is great for the area, and you'll have all the advantages of the other types as well. The main advantage of Fortune's is the October bloom. Small tubular flowers are borne in clusters along the branches in mid- to late-October. These delightful, sweet-smelling blooms are hard to see, but remarkably scented. When all else is fading in the fall landscape, your Fortune's will be alive and fragrant for several weeks.

A real safe bet for the coastal garden, grow your Fortune's in a sunny to partially shaded spot with moderate amounts of mulch, rich soil that's well-drained and a neutral pH. Be careful of the spines on the leaves and allow plenty of room for growth. This plant is a sure winner for evergreen foliage and years of carefree pleasure. If you don't prune it every year, it will reach a height of ten feet and a width of six feet.

MONTH-BY-MONTH GUIDE FOR FORTUNE'S OSMANTHUS

JANUARY	Some copper-colored foliage is not a major problem during the coldest times of the year.
FEBRUARY-MARCH	Bring a few green branches inside as a reminder that some plants are green during the winter months.
APRIL	Your plant will begin to push some new growth. New leaves are pale and wilt easily. Water is essential on windy, warm days.
MAY	Growth continues, but resist pruning 'til you see the way your plant will perform as the new leaves "harden off."
JUNE-AUGUST	In mid-June, apply a cup of bloodmeal around the base of your plant. White, foamy secretions along the branches indicate some minor insects that rarely cause problems. In late July, you can prune as needed, but don't prune too deeply. Tip pruning is always best so you'll preserve the shape of the plant.
SEPTEMBER	Test the soil and replace the mulch. Make sure your plant has plenty of water. Buds will be forming along the branches.
OCTOBER	Blooming can take place quickly. The fragrance is quite pronounced. Honey bees are obvious.
NOVEMBER	As blooming halts, growth and performance will slow down now as the fall season gets under way.
DECEMBER	The holly-like foliage reminds some folks of the coming holidays. A few branches in a vase will last a week or ten days.

Philadelphus coronarius

Sweet Mock Orange

'*Aureus*'   The variety most sought. Plenty of four-petaled flowers from a fountain of foliage. It is heavily scented with orange. A vigorous grower reaching ten feet in a single season. An old South favorite.

'*Variegatus*'   Green leaves are tipped in white. The variegated form of '*Aureus*', this ornamental offers all the characteristics of '*Aureus*' with a little more show. Often difficult to find in ordinary nurseries, so order ahead.

The genus has a number of species many of which are highly fragrant, but none like sweet mock orange. Oddly enough, it is so named not for its fragrance, but for its petal shape which resembles that of any citrus plant. A wonderful bonus, though, is the intense aroma. You should smell this plant before you buy it, because the fragrance may be too strong! This delightful plant is a very aggressive grower, quickly expanding to ten or more feet in a single season, and should be used as a specimen in the garden, allowed to stand alone, or in a mixed bed with other upright plants so that its graceful arches can expand around and through the branches of other shrubs. It makes a fine addition to a group of oleanders, and mixed with kerria or osmanthus, it can be a stunning addition to your ornamental flower bed. Mock orange tends to get leggy, so prune at will as soon as it finishes its blooming cycle which will take place in early spring just after it foliates. The plant is deciduous and is ideal for forcing in a cool location. Ordinary soil is perfect, and your *Philadelphus coronarius* will be maintenance-free. Be careful where you plant it though, and allow plenty of room for expansion.

This plant likes the sunshine and will not tolerate poorly drained soil.

(Note: there are a number of plants in the Southern landscape that are called "mock orange." When you visit the nursery, it is always helpful to know the botanical name of the plant you are seeking, especially in this case.)

MONTH-BY-MONTH GUIDE FOR SWEET MOCK ORANGE

JANUARY	Your plant is dormant.
FEBRUARY-MARCH	Adequate water is a must, even though the plant has no leaves. Protect from damaging weather, especially ice build-up.
APRIL	Pale leaves appear in the eyes of the branches. A late freeze may nip some of this new foliage. Flower buds appear and some flowers may appear.
MAY	Your plant will bloom completely anytime this month. New foliage appears, strong stem growth takes place, and the plant will acquire new shoots many of which will increase the arching of the plant substantially.
JUNE	Prune unwanted growth and check the size of the plant with careful, selective cutting. This new growth will support next May's flowers.
JULY-SEPTEMBER	No special attention is required, though general maintenance is always needed. Water is essential as new growth continues. The "dog days" will slow the plant's activity.
OCTOBER-NOVEMBER	Dormancy approaches, some leaf loss occurs, and the foliage changes color. Apply a cup or two of Greensand around the drip line.
DECEMBER	Complete dormancy is evident now as the plant loses all its leaves. Rake around the plant and apply fresh mulch. Water deeply before the first freeze.

Pinus thunburgiana

Japanese black pine

Though this area has an abundance of native pines, this cultivated variety fits a number of needs for the ornamental garden, and if you like the appearance of pine trees but don't want the height and size of our natives, then Japanese black pine can offer lots of advantages.

Native to Japan, it has a twisted growth habit with rich-textured bark and will grow as high as fifty feet, though most don't reach that size. The needles are short clusters of two-to-four inch leaves which are stiff and pale green. The small cones are abundant and appear in all seasons.

This tree tolerates salt spray very well, and is useful along the beachfront or in windswept areas. Plant it as a specimen or in groups beside buildings or in the open yard. It has no pests, withstands drought and needs no fertilization and little maintenance.

MONTH-BY-MONTH GUIDE FOR JAPANESE BLACK PINE

JANUARY-FEBRUARY	The tree is dormant. Notice the twisted growth habit and obvious cones. Dark green bundles of short needles are obvious.
MARCH-APRIL	Some new growth may appear as the spring season approaches.
MAY-AUGUST	You can prune any unwanted growth during this period.
SEPTEMBER-OCTOBER	As fall comes in, your pine may need some pruning or limb removal to balance the tree and to remove unwanted growth.
NOVEMBER-DECEMBER	When all else in the dormant landscape is bare, your pine will stay green. Birds will nest in the branches.

Pines of all species are adapted to the coastal Carolinas. Long leaf pine is pictured here.

Pittosporum tobira

Pittosporum

The species is often called "mock orange" because of the lovely white, star-shaped flowers that bloom in spring. Long-lasting and highly fragrant, these flowers age to a creamy color which actually enhances the appearance of the shrub as they develop. Many homeowners never experience the beauty of the flowers, however, because "pitts" as they are often called, have such an aggressive growth habit, folks tend to prune them often, thus cutting out the flower buds which are set soon after the plant blooms. It's a tough choice for gardeners, because this plant, like so many that grow well here along our section of the coast, requires some pruning if it is to remain a part of our well-tended landscape. But if an annual shearing can be done, and the plant can be left to grow unchecked for a full season, you'll have lots of flowers from this handsome shrub. It is often sold as Japanese pittosporum, and is offered in a variegated plant with white-on-green foliage, in pure green and as a dwarf type. Cold hardy, disease-resistant and tough, this plant has some wonderful characteristics. It can be held as a well-rounded, small shrub by annual pruning or shearing or it can be allowed to develop as a full-sized plant, reaching its maximum height of six feet with a spread of four feet. Grown beneath windows, it can quickly scent the entire house on a warm spring morning. It offers cover for small birds, shade for low-growing border plants, excellent foliage for seasonal cutting and a cool background for annual and perennial color gardens. The plant will tolerate a wide range of soil conditions, but wet soil will cause problems over time.

Partial shade is best, but full shade is acceptable, though plants grown in full shade tend to be thinner and have fewer flowers. Pruning can be done at any time. Older plants can be headed back to within a foot or two of the base, and recovery is quite rapid.

You won't have many problems with this plant, though it benefits from annual feeding. High acid soil causes a definite chlorotic appearance.

An excellent selection for a dwarfed, low growing pittosporum is 'Wheeler's Dwarf', though it is less cold resistant than others.

The late Jim Ferger, a well-recognized coastal horticulturist, referred to pittosporum as "the most complete plant in the coastal garden."

MONTH-BY-MONTH GUIDE FOR PITTOSPORUM

JANUARY	The dormant plant will show some flower buds in the tips of the leaf whorls.
FEBRUARY-MARCH	Protect your plant from severe cold and windy weather.
APRIL-MAY	Blooming can occur anytime now. Prune your plant only to remove damaged or unwanted growth.
MAY-JUNE	As soon as new growth "hardens," prune or shear, depending on the growth habit you desire. If the plant doesn't revive quickly, make sure water is sufficient, and fertilize with one application of tankage at the rate of one cup per three feet of height, raked into the soil around the base and watered well.
JULY-SEPTEMBER	Treat for scale if needed by using a horticultural oil spray. Prune excessive growth as needed, but be careful not to remove too much top growth as flower buds are forming.
OCTOBER-NOVEMBER	Replace the mulch with clean, dry material, and check the soil pH. Amend it accordingly.
DECEMBER	Your plant is dormant, though mild weather may result in some slight, pale growth.

Pyrus calleryana 'Bradford'

Bradford pear

No shade tree in the coastal area has enjoyed as much popularity as this one, and the reasons are obvious. It provides dramatic appearances in all the seasons. In the spring, it shows dynamic flowering with clouds of white flowers along bare branches, followed by a profusion of dark green leaves that cover the broad, balanced canopy. In the summer, the shade from 'Bradford' is lush and cool, and in the fall, the color is fantastic as the leaves change from green to deep orange-red and remain on the tree for several weeks. It makes a perfect winter tree with its bare branches lining the skyline. Pest-free with little or no fertilization needed, it has few requirements.

'Bradford' is not without some drawbacks. Usually sold as a graft, the trunk has some thick, low-growing branches which can split quickly in a fall storm. It's probably best to prune these away as the tree matures. The wood is brittle, and if it breaks, pruning it may destroy the basic pyramid shape. It is not resistant to some blight disorders and may have to be treated with fungicides in the summer or early fall.

Plant this tree in an isolated place so it can grow to its full height and spread, upwards to fifty feet and outward nearly as much. It grows rapidly and often flowers in the first several years. Plan for future growth, and though it can be planted in rows or with other Bradfords, it makes a fine specimen in the open landscape. The fruit is an insignificant berry that resembles a small pear, borne in clusters at the ends of the flowering-fruiting spurs.

MONTH-BY-MONTH GUIDE FOR BRADFORD PEAR

JANUARY-FEBRUARY	The tree is dormant. Look for storm damage among the branches and prune it away.
MARCH	Flowering is a month or so away, and you can apply a light application of fertilizer late in the month. Make sure the tree has enough water (half an inch every three days) to support the dynamic blooming habit.
APRIL	Early in the month the tree will show some flowers. As the days get warmer, the entire tree will burst into bloom with clouds of white flowers which last a week or so.
MAY	As the flowers fade and the foliage appears, now is a good time to do some light pruning. Try to avoid too much cutting as the shape of the tree is important.
JUNE-AUGUST	Look for blighted leaves which appear scorched, pale and discolored. Treat the tree with a basic fungicide late in the day if you notice a significant problem. Fruits may appear.
SEPTEMBER-OCTOBER	Fall approaches and the tree may stop growing and begin to change color. Late in the period, full color change will begin with a wonderful show of red and orange leaves. Birds will eat the fruit.
NOVEMBER	Color change may linger as the leaves begin to fall. If you have noticed disease during the summer, it is crucial to rake well beneath the tree and destroy the fallen foliage. Keep the base of the tree clean. No mulch is required, but younger trees will benefit from a light application of compost around the base.
DECEMBER	Prune now, especially unbalanced branches and lower limbs which may split away in spring storms.

Prunus caroliniana

Carolina cherrylaurel

The genus *Prunus* contains a very large number of plants, including all the cherries, plums, apricots, peaches and almonds. Some of the world's favorite cultivated shrubs and trees are in the family. For example, the Yoshino cherries on the Mall in Washington, D.C., the delightful myrobalan plum, the stunning evergreen beauty English laurel (*P. laurocerasus*), and a wonderful shrub for the coastal South, a Japanese apricot called 'Omoi-no-mama' are all members of the *Prunus* family. Here we have a rather plain shrub in Carolina cherrylaurel as compared to its cousins, but the utility of the plant is a great advantage. NC State University lists no pests for this maintenance-free plant which grows to a height of thirty feet with a spreading crown of rich green foliage. It can be sheared or pruned, or it can be left completely alone for tall, arching growth. Known for its pollen output in the spring, the plant sports a lot of fragrant, spire-like creamy white flowers. The resulting fruit is a cherry-like black berry much desired by wildlife. The seeds sprout readily from bird droppings. This is a quick-growing shrub, ideal for partial shade or sunny locations

and an excellent choice for any soil condition. It is very useful for screening buildings, as a hedge, as a fence covering and for property borders. It is ideal for shading outbuildings. This is a native plant.

MONTH-BY-MONTH GUIDE FOR CAROLINA CHERRYLAUREL

JANUARY	Your dormant plant will have a bronzed-purple cast this month as cold weather causes some damage to foliage, and nutrients are "locked up" in cold soil.
FEBRUARY-MARCH	The cherrylaurel is one of the first landscape plants to break dormancy. Look for flowers and new growth. Feed your plant with a cup of tankage before Easter.
APRIL-MAY	A period of quick growth will take place, and you can control unwanted growth by pruning or shearing as required.
JUNE-JULY	Steady growth continues now as summer moves along, and you can push your plant a little harder by repeating the fertilizer application.
AUGUST	Seeds develop and your plant will slow down for a while as heat dormancy takes over.
SEPTEMBER-NOVEMBER	A period of rapid growth may take place, fruit develops and the shrub begins dormancy. Prune at will.
DECEMBER	Your plant is dormant.

Prunus serrulata 'Kwanzan'

Kwanzan oriental cherry

One of the most popular of the many cultivated varieties of Oriental cherries, this small tree is particularly nice for small spaces. It grows to thirty feet at maturity, can often have multi-trunks, but is usually found as a graft with a single trunk. The leaves are large, double-toothed and rich green, though they can have a slight bronze cast when opening. They are produced after the flowers in the early spring. 'Kwanzan' is a little later in blooming than most cherries, but the flowers are worth the wait. Large, rose-pink with thirty petals, they can often exceed two inches across. If you want a shaded small area, this tree is perfect, and the size makes it ideal for a patio garden. The fall color, though not remarkable, is quite pleasant.

'Kwanzan' is not without a few problems, the least of which is that it has been used extensively in many commercial and residential plantings. Galls can develop along the branches as the result of fungal attacks, and the tree can become misshapen with the loss of limbs. Since the vase shape of the tree is important, 'Kwanzans' which have become distorted can be unpleasant. To be on the safe side, preventive care is necessary to guarantee years of quality growth, so follow the guideline carefully.

MONTH-BY-MONTH GUIDE FOR KWANZAN ORIENTAL CHERRY

JANUARY	Look for damaged limbs and broken branches in your dormant tree.
FEBRUARY 25TH	If today is not wet and cloudy, spray it with a basic fruit tree spray which contains a broad base of pesticides.
MARCH	Flower buds will be forming now as the spring season approaches.
APRIL	Flowering can take place any time now as the days get warmer and longer. As the petals fall, rake beneath the tree often.
MAY-JUNE	Avoid pruning, but if you notice diseased branches, prune them away quickly.
JULY-AUGUST	Prune any parts of the tree that need maintenance, though be cautious not to distort the basic shape of the tree. Good watering techniques and fresh mulch are essential. Keep the lawn grass fertilizers away from the base of the tree.
SEPTEMBER-OCTOBER	If you notice sappy discharge, swelling or splitting of the wood or other signs of distress, apply a single dose of dormant horticultural oil to the entire tree, particularly the wood.
DECEMBER	Rake beneath the tree to collect all fallen leaves, replace the mulch with fresh material and check the soil pH early in the month. Amend the soil as needed.

Prunus yedoensis

Yoshino cherry

This may be the most spectacular of the ornamental cherries because of its magnificent early display of white or blush-pink flowers in spring. This is the famous tree of the nation's capital, and has been widely planted as a specimen tree in many of the coastal area's premier landscapes.

A Japanese native, it's a hybrid and does not exist in the wild. The origins are unclear, but Yoshino cherries have been around for many years, even though the life span is only twenty-five to thirty years.

This tree will grow quickly in just about any location, and from the first year or so, you can count on clouds of white or light pink raceme-like flowers with a slight powdery fragrance. The canopy can be dense with plenty of dark, deeply-toothed leaves which turn a pale gold color in the fall, rapidly dropping as winter approaches.

The Yoshino is strong, hardy and pest-free and requires little maintenance. If you are looking for one shade-flowering-fall-colored tree for your garden, this is the one. There are several cultivars, but any good nurseryman will direct you to the right choice if you simply ask for the species hybrid. A mature tree reaches sixty-five feet in height and will spread a broad canopy at least that much

Over the years, this tree will become one of your favorites.

MONTH-BY-MONTH GUIDE FOR YOSHINO CHERRY

JANUARY	Look for damaged or broken limbs, and prune them out of your dormant tree.
FEBRUARY	As the month moves along, water your tree and replace the mulch.
MARCH	Flowers can erupt at any time. A few sunny mild days will send your cherry into full blossoming.
APRIL	Prune away crossed branches and unwanted growth as soon as flowering is complete. Though the spent flowers are a wonderful sight as they fall, many blooms will linger for several days.
JUNE-SEPTEMBER	Summer requires little maintenance, but make sure the tree is watered in dry periods. Replace the mulch around Labor Day.
NOVEMBER	As soon as leaf loss is complete, check your tree for signs of borers. Do you see any pin holes? Dead branches? If so a single application of fruit tree spray will solve the problem.
DECEMBER	Rake up the fallen leaves and replace or add clean mulch around the shallow roots.

Punica grenatum

Pomegranate

Each fall, most of us are treated to pomegranates in the markets, either for actual table use, or for holiday decorations. But it is quite easy to grow this ornamental shrub and have the bonus of the fruit directly from your home garden fruit area or ornamental plant bed.

The genus, *Punica*, contains only a few species, *grenatum* being the most popular. The plant is deciduous, but foliates quickly in the spring. It throws a long series of tubular, crape-like orange flowers which mature in late summer and early fall as the pomegranate fruits—the red and orange spheres filled with hundreds of sour-sweet seeds and red juice which call to mind the old-fashioned days of open air markets or exotic fruits from tropical zones.

Pomegranates thrive in our warm coastal climate, and require very little attention. They like sunny, protected locations in just about any soil type, and will tolerate a broad pH range. They are well suited for hedge work, in natural settings, or even as free standing plants featured in the central landscape. They also mix well with other edible plants in a fruit or berry section of the garden.

The ornamental varieties of this species have extra-large double, red-orange flowers which do not bear fruit but offer a spectacular show. The dwarf variety, *P.grenatum nana,* is a low grower with the same flower color and foliage as the larger version, but with smaller fruits. It grows only eighteen inches tall, while the large plant will grow up to six feet.

For variety, color, interesting texture and uncommon attraction, find a well-drained, protected spot in your yard for this old-fashioned, revived classic.

MONTH-BY-MONTH GUIDE FOR POMEGRANATE

JANUARY	The dormant plant has lost its leaves for the season.
FEBRUARY-MARCH	Change the mulch, and in early March, spray the dormant shrub with a horticultural oil spray.
APRIL	Foliage appears along the branches as the shrub breaks dormancy. Help it along if you think it needs it with a single application of 5-10-10 at the rate of one-fourth cup per two feet of growth.
MAY	Flowers appear this month and will continue for several weeks. Water your plant so that it gets one-half inch every other day, and apply fresh mulch around the base of the shrub. Test the soil and amend it to a neutral pH.
JUNE	Flowering stops, but you may notice some fruit forming where the tubular flowers were. Remember that double flowering varieties do not set fruit.
JULY-AUGUST	Your plant is mostly pest-free, but pay close attention to water requirements as the red-orange fruits continue to form. You may need to support the heavier branches by staking or trellissing.
SEPTEMBER-OCTOBER	Fruit matures now as the days get longer. Some foliage will fall and you may notice some color change in the leaves from green to yellow or orange-red.
NOVEMBER	The fruit ripens and matures completely now, and may fall from the shrub. Look for red, orange and mottled spheres with a tough, shiny outer shell. Good sanitation is important. It is achieved by raking beneath the shrub and harvesting the fruits often.
DECEMBER	The amazing growth season for this plant is over now, and dormancy sets in for the winter.

Pyracantha

Firethorn, Red pyracantha

[Note: In this section we'll discuss two different species of plants.]

There are two species of pyracantha that perform well in the coastal area of southeastern North Carolina, both of which contain quite a few named cultivars. But don't expect the local nursery to get too involved in the differences between the two, the advantages of one over the other, or which one produces a better plant. To many, it is not worth the confusion because the two species are very closely related. Nonetheless, this special microclimate in which we live has a direct bearing on pyracanthas, and for that reason, we'll just take a closer look at the these two species. In so doing, you might be a little better prepared when you start shopping the local nurseries or garden centers for the best pyracantha for your landscape.

P. coccinea   Here's the firethorn that is perfect for espalier. We see this species frequently, and it is easily recognized by the dense, bushy growth and abundance of thorns. Plenty of five-petaled flowers in spring eventually produce mounds of orange-red fruits on lush shrubs.

'Navaho'   A cold-resistant, pest-resistant variety. Nice round shape with orange fruit. Grows wider rather than taller.

'Lalandei'   A choice firethorn. Robust growth up to fifteen feet. Very popular, very strong, very productive.

'Teton'   Grow this shrub for yellow fruit, and if you want a plant that is tall, slender and not so wide.

P. koidzumii   This species was once considered the best of the lot to grow along the coast, and its related hybrids are among the the finest examples of firethorn available. This is the famous Formosa firethorn. It is very heat and drought tolerant, and is often preferred over varieties of *P. coccinea* because of its colorful fruit.

'Victory'   Dark red berries last for months on this arching, heavily thorned, woody shrub. Thick foliage pushes an upright habit to fifteen feet.

'Santa Cruz'   A strong ground cover that requires little care.

The story is often told about the fellow who went to the nursery and requested a look at the Pyracanthas in hopes of buying one. The nurseryman was quick to ask why he would want to! Those who have cultivated this interesting shrub know very well its disadvantages. It is impossible to penetrate, it is very difficult to handle, and pruning can be done only from a distance, using loppers, and a good pair of thick leather gloves. All of this, of course, because of the thorns that cover the branches and stems, thus the name "firethorn." If anything good can be found in growing it, the thorns may actually contribute because the plant makes an excellent barrier and hedge. Beside that, the flowers in spring are profuse and fragrant, and the resulting red or orange berries are a wonderful addition to the fall and winter landscape. Some selections are good for espalier, others make good groundcovers, and all should be left alone with as little pruning as possible. Firethorns have only a few pests. Lacebugs will devour the foliage quickly if left unattended, so treat them with pyrethrins. A fungal condition called "fire blight" will discolor the foliage, and it can be easily controlled with a basic garden fungicide. Grow your plant in a sunny spot, well drained soil which is rich in humus, and make sure the pH of the soil is neutral. If you must prune, cut the plant back at any time. You'll lose some berries, but new growth will develop rapidly.

Most firethorns will exceed fifteen feet if allowed to grow at will and can ramble for as many as twenty feet. The lower growers are bred to spread and grow more slowly, but even they have a dynamic growth habit. Plant your selection in a location that will allow plenty of room, preferably against a wall or structure. They lack the ability to cling, so you'll have to help them hold onto an object.

MONTH-BY-MONTH GUIDE FOR FIRETHORN

JANUARY	Though dormant, your plant will have some persistent berries and foliage. Towards the end of the month apply a cup of superphosphate around the drip line and scratch it into the soil.
FEBRUARY-MARCH	Little care is needed. If your plant is espalliered, check your ties and hangers.
APRIL-MAY	Foliage will push up from the terminal ends, and some flowering will take place. By the end of May, the whole plant will bloom with lots of fragrant flowers. As soon as blooming is complete, some light pruning is okay if needed.
JUNE-JULY	Some branches may become leggy, so you'll have to prune for maintenance. Keep the fungicide handy for treatment of blight. Berries are forming.
AUGUST-SEPTEMBER	Fresh mulch will help the plant stay cool.
OCTOBER-NOVEMBER	Fruit begins to ripen, foliage is lush and green, and you should be seeing a healthy, colorful plant. Lacebugs may be a problem, so keep a watchful eye as dormancy approaches.
DECEMBER	Dormancy takes over, but the fruit is ripe and wildlife is abundant. Your plant is in prime time now for berry display and dark green foliage.

Quercus virginiana

Live oak

This tree is called live oak because it is evergreen. Once used for ship-building, furniture, jewelers' blocks and mallets, the tree was heavily harvested in colonial times. Native Americans used the roots for dye and the bark as a treatment for malaria. In the 1800s, public lands were purchased to preserve this valuable species.

Though the tree seldom reaches heights greater than sixty feet, it has a broad spread with a dense crown that can exceed a hundred feet at maturity. The trunk and buttress flare are the largest of any native tree, and can reach four or five feet in diameter. Spanish moss is attracted to the tree which adds to the Southern charm of this oak as it ages. The bark becomes deeply furrowed and rough as the tree ages.

Live oaks produce acorns which mature in the fall. They are a valuable part of the mast. In the spring, older leaves fall to the ground as new foliage appears. Raking is difficult because the leaves are slippery and tough.

This is a massive tree that acquires great character, shape and distinction as it matures. A slow-grower, it reaches full size many years after planting, and you should cultivate a live oak with future generations in mind. A similar species, *Quercus laurifolia*, 'Darlington,' (Darlington Oak) is a faster growing tree that offers many of the characteristics of live oak.

Plant this tree in sandy soil and allow plenty of room for it to expand over the years. The lower branches will grow almost horizontally and will shade plants which grow beneath them. Azaleas make excellent companions for live oaks.

MONTH-BY-MONTH GUIDE FOR LIVE OAK

JANUARY-MARCH	During the dormant season the live oak is still green.
APRIL-MAY	As new leaves sprout along the branches, the previous season's growth will shed. Raking is a difficult chore, and you may want to wait until all the leaves are down before you take on the task.
JUNE-JULY	New growth continues and acorns may develop.
AUGUST-OCTOBER	The late summer is a wonderful season for live oaks. Spanish moss with drape the branches, and the tree makes an excellent habitat for wildlife.
OCTOBER-DECEMBER	Some leaf loss will take place during the fall, but not as much as in the spring. Acorns will fall to the ground, but the tree will keep most of its foliage. As other trees lose their leaves and the landscape becomes dormant, the live oak will remain a featured part of your landscape.

Rhaphiolepis indica

Indian hawthorne

Indian hawthornes gained popularity in the coastal area of the Atlantic South in the early 1970s because of their durability, maintenance-free growth style, flowers and foliage. But as they became more widely used, their distinction as a species became confused with *R. umbellata*, a very similar species. Now horticulturists find it very difficult to distinguish between the two, especially because there are several named cultivated varieties. Don't be surprised if the "tell-tag" on a plant you think is *R.indica* is labeled as *R. umbellata*. In any case, rest assured that the difference is miniscule, and if you purchase Indian hawthorne or *Yeddo rhaphiolepis*, you are getting a plant that is culturally equal.

This is the plant that has been featured in nearly every landscape design possible, from commercial bulk plantings to natural settings in distinctive homesites. Some say that Indian hawthornes are overused, but if they are it is because they have been featured in gardens "up front" where they are so highly visible. Use them in massed groups, along walls and in hedges, and you'll be more than pleased with their carefree style and generous growth habit. Four or five hours of sunshine daily, well-drained soil, good fertilization and slightly acidic pH should generate an excellent stand of Indian hawthornes. Even though they are quite common, they are worth a spot in your garden, especially if they are healthy and vigorous. Grow them for fragrance, color and vibrant leathery foliage and a considerable amount of maintenance-free pleasure.

The growth habit is similar to kurume azaleas. Most varieties will reach about twenty-two inches and spread about the same width, though some selections will exceed that size. Be sure to ask your nurseryman about the specific growth habit of the plant you are selecting.

MONTH-BY-MONTH GUIDE FOR INDIAN HAWTHORNE

JANUARY	Your plant is dormant. See some purple colored foliage? This is normal, as are the remaining black fruits that have persisted since late summer.
FEBRUARY	Around Valentine's Day, apply a light dose of superphosphate around the base of each plant.
MARCH	Fertilize each plant with a premium grade 8-8-8 fertilizer, at a fourth cup per plant. Water each plant well during the growing season. Replace the mulch.
APRIL	After the azaleas bloom, your Indian hawthornes will begin to show some signs of dormancy break. Blooms may appear at anytime. Look for five-petaled, white flowers with pink centers, good fragrance and renewed growth. Keep the weeds away from your plants.
MAY	Some blooming may persist, but as soon as it stops, prune at will, especially excessive growth from the preceding season.
JUNE	Test the soil and adjust the pH accordingly. It is really important to grow your Indian hawthorne in soil that has the correct pH.
JULY-AUGUST	Don't let your plants dry out. Half an inch of water every three days is essential now as your plants set the buds for next year's blossoms.
SEPTEMBER 15th	Apply half a cup of superphosphate, half a cup of Epsom salts and spray each plant with horticultural oil spray.
OCTOBER-NOVEMBER	Freshen the mulch, and now is a good time to root prune the plant if needed.
DECEMBER	Lethargic appearance indicates dormancy. Don't be surprised to see some leaf discoloration and "sleepy" habit.

Rhododendron indicum

Indian azalea, Indica azalea

'George Lindley Taber'   Perhaps the most popular of the hybrids. Pink flowers with a deep blotch make this the dazzler of the azalea bed.

'Mrs. G.G.Gerbing'   White flowers with a green eye, crisp and brilliant against pale foliage.

'Formosa'   The standard by which azaleas are judged. Big and robust, these deep purple flowers are the pride of the Southern garden.

'Pride of Mobile'   A rosy-pink flower, as big as 'Formosa' but slightly longer-lasting with deep green foliage. A bit later than the others.

Years ago, botanists reclassified azaleas to include them in the genus with rhododendrons, now making this genus one of the largest. Azaleas are the most popular of the garden plants. They are grown in all fifty states, many of which promote the plants as a leading nursery product. The indica hybrids were developed in South Carolina in the early 1800s, but it is suspected that Orton Plantation played a large role in developing them as a major Southern landscape plant. Hundred-year-old plants thrive in Oakdale Cemetery in Wilmington as well as the historical districts, and many specimen plants can be found in ordinary places. Though encyclopedias have been written on the culture of these vastly popular plants, the general planting and care for indica hybrids is quite simple. The "show off" plants perform best in dappled sunlight which is filtered through light shade. Plant your azalea in rich, slightly acid soil and never let it dry out. The root system is shallow, so avoid cultivating or applying herbicides anywhere near the root zone. The plants that flower best are those that receive plenty of water during the heat of the summer months.

The indica hybrids are the tallest growing azaleas in cultivation. They will exceed six feet in good conditions and spread over a five foot area.

MONTH-BY-MONTH GUIDE FOR INDICA AZALEAS

JANUARY	Your plant is dormant.
FEBRUARY 25th	Rake away the mulch around the base of your plant and apply one-fourth cup of superphosphate around the drip line. Replace the mulch only if it is dry and clean.
MARCH 15-30	During this period, fertilize your plant with one-fourth cup of 6-6-12 fertilizer and one-fourth cup Epsom salts. Spray your plant with a basic garden fungicide following the label instructions carefully.
APRIL	Your plant will bloom this month. As soon as buds become obvious, rake away and destroy all mulch. Water from the bottom only...no splashing! No fertilizers, but once during the blooming cycle, spray the plant early one morning with a garden fungicide.
MAY	Do not allow spent or dead blossoms to collect around the plant. Rake and mow regularly. Any pruning should be done as soon as blooming stops. This is the best month to prune.
JUNE-AUGUST	Water is important now as the buds set-up for next year. Half an inch every three days is about right. No pruning, no feeding, but watch for insects.
SEPTEMBER-OCTOBER	Mulch the base of your plant with fresh, clean pine straw. Get a soil test to determine the pH and before October thirtieth apply one fourth cup of superphosphate around each plant.
NOVEMBER-DECEMBER	Some yellow or copper foliage is normal. Keep a watchful eye for severe weather, and protect your prized plants from winter injury.

Rhododendron obtusum

Kurume azalea

This wonderful race of azaleas probably originated high in the mountains of Japan. Little is known of their ancestry, or how they arrived in America, though it is suspected that they came to the colonies from Europe. Once established in the colonies, they quickly became one of the most popular garden plants, showing up in established gardens early in the colonial period. Today there are hundreds of cultivars and more being developed all the time.

Kurumes are prized plants because of their growth habit, their remarkable color show and their resistance to pests. They don't have the cultural problems that plague many other landscape ornamentals. Often the first plants to show color in the spring, they might throw a flower on the first warm day of March and they are often the last plants blooming when azalea season stops.

Though they have a growth habit somewhat slower than the Indian azaleas, they develop much denser and rounder plants. The leaves are smaller than indicas, the flowers are more compact, and they usually stop growing at eight or ten feet.

They should not be pruned, so place them in the garden where they will grow and develop naturally. They make fine hedges, are excellent in massed beds, and a group of them can be displayed in the open lawn. Natural settings are ideal locations for kurumes. Like all azaleas, they prefer slightly acid soil, and a well-drained, partially shaded location. Since the roots are close to the surface, be careful how you cultivate around them.

'Coral Bells'   The most popular of the kurumes. Powdery-pink, loaded with flowers and a dense growth habit.

'Snow'   Pure white, early flowers and very lush.

'Hino Crimson'   Brilliant red flowers and a massive growth habit.

'Hinodegiri'   Rose-red flowers cover this exceptional, well-mounded azalea. Very striking.

'Red Wing'   True scarlet. This little known variety could be the envy of the neighborhood.

'Salmon Bells'   The salmon variety of 'Coral Bells'. Not pink, not peach-colored, but an unusual combination of the two.

MONTH-BY-MONTH GUIDE FOR KURUME AZALEA

JANUARY	Your plant is dormant.
FEBRUARY 25TH	Rake away the mulch from the base of the plant and apply one- quarter cup of superphosphate around the drip line. Replace the mulch with clean, dry material.
MARCH 15TH- 30TH	Fertilize now with one-quarter cup of 5-10-10 fertilizer and one-quarter cup of Epsom salts for each plant, scratched into the soil around the base. Though kurumes are generally free from fungal diseases, you may notice some petal blight. This will appear as greasy looking flowers or petals which turn brown and fall from the plant. If this happens, apply a basic fungicide to the entire plant following the label directions carefully. Blooms may appear any time this month.
APRIL	This is the peak blooming period. Rake away the mulch as soon as blossoms appear. Water from the ground up with no splashing. Keep the base of the plant clear.
MAY	Do not allow spent blossoms to collect around the plant. Rake and mow regularly. Avoid pruning, but if you think it's necessary, prune as soon as blooming stops.
JUNE-AUGUST	Water is important now as the buds for next year's flowers are being set. Keep the weeds down and watch for caterpillars.
SEPTEMBER-OCTOBER	Mulch the plant with fresh, clean pine straw. Test the soil's pH and amend accordingly. In the final week of October, apply a quarter cup of superphosphate around the base of each plant.
NOVEMBER-DECEMBER	Some yellow or copper-colored foliage is normal as dormancy approaches. Some azaleas are deciduous and may lose foliage this period. Protect your prize plants from winter damage.

Rosa

Hybrid rose

The world of roses is quite complex, and this often intimidates folks into thinking that roses cannot be grown in the coastal area of the South without huge effort. Actually, this is not entirely true, because some types of roses can be grown quite easily, while others will thrive with just a little effort.

There are far too many types and methods for us to address here; however, let's look at some types of roses, how they are classed and a little about care and maintenance. The chart will show how and when to fertilize, prune and winterize.

The late Roy Hennesy, a rose grower from the Pacific Northwest, encouraged folks to grow roses not for the challenge they offer, not for the remarkable experience of accomplishing a blue ribbon bloom, not even for the fragrance that has captivated the world for centuries. He encouraged folks to simply grow roses for their pleasure, and without complicating the effort too much, enjoying whatever opportunities came along.

Good advice from Dr. Hennesy. The key here along the warm, humid coast is to keep the maintenance schedule on track.

Types of Roses

These are a bit confusing because they overlap, but these classifications have been created by and for gardeners to help them understand the divisions and categories. Categories change, as do descriptions, but these divisions seem to remain consistent over the years.

HYBRID TEAS   What the world thinks a rose ought to look like. Plant this type if you have room enough for only one rose. These roses are showy but difficult to raise and are susceptible to many diseases and insects.

FLORIBUNDAS   Low-growing shrubs that have clustered blooms. Similar to teas, they may bloom only once in the early spring.

GRANDIFLORAS   A class created in 1949 to accommodate a single type, "Queen Elizabeth ." These are very similar to teas.

MINIATURES   Dwarf varieties of any rose. Often as hardy, but sometimes not as fragrant or dynamic as their larger cousins.

SPECIES ROSES   The original of the originals. They always bloom from single flowers with five petals. They produce true from seed, are thornless and climbing and are prized for their hips. The hybrids from this class include the celebrated rugosa types which, though heavily thorned as a result of their hybridization, have become so popular as coastal Carolina garden roses.

ANTIQUES   These are the leftovers from previous generations of breeding and experimentation. A huge group, it includes cabbage type roses, the European Provence roses, China roses and old tea roses, the forerunners of modern teas. The antiques are highly prized today as collectors' roses in old world gardens.

CLIMBERS   No rose actually "climbs" because they lack the tendrils for clinging, so we have to help them along by providing support as we tie them to trellises and arbors. But this rather complicated group includes ramblers and roadside runners which scamper over fences and hedges. Some bloom only once, some bloom all summer. Many climbers bloom from two-year-old canes only, so pruning them becomes complicated. This is the category that includes the *Kordesii* Climbers, named for the botanist William Kordes. These fascinating roses are prized garden beauties. Also included in this group are the "Cherokee" roses, so obvious along the rural fence lines of coastal Carolina. Cherokees have very delicate, light pink flowers with prominent stamens, and are extremely vigorous.

MONTH BY MONTH GUIDE FOR ROSES

JANUARY	The plant is dormant.
FEBRUARY	Pay some attention to your plant this month. Remove any sucker growth that remains, and clean up around the base of the plant. Make a note about unusual sightings or conditions.
MARCH	Prepare for spring break this month with good clean up and sanitation. Replace the mulch and on the twentieth, fertilize each plant with one-fourth cup of 8-8-8, one-fourth cup of Epsom salts, one-fourth cup of superphosphate, and one-fourth cup of bloodmeal. Scatter this mixture around the base of each plant, and then apply a gallon or two of fresh garden compost around the base of each plant as a mulch. Water the plant deeply.
APRIL	Growth now begins with strong production from the earlier feeding. Blooming is on the way. An application of a basic insecticide around the base of the plant may help in controlling insects. Spray the soil around the base of each plant with a basic garden fungicide. Set Japanese beetle traps in plants away from your roses, and keep the insecticides handy in case of attacks. Every ten days, apply a light dose of fungicide over the entire plant, including stems, leaves and soil.
MAY-JULY	Blooming continues from the hybrid types, but the ramblers and climbers may be finished. Old garden roses are about to burst into new growth cycles. Protect your plants from insects. Black spot, a fungal disease that turns foliage to a yellow color with circular brown and black spots becomes a problem now as the "dog days" bring on the humidity of late summer. This period of the summer may trigger some dormancy and blooming may slow. Good air circulation is a must. Keep up a good watch for disease, and be prepared to apply fungicides as needed. Fertilize every four weeks with 5-10-10. Water regularly, up to two inches weekly. Harvest flowers often by cutting the stems as deeply as possible. The cut flowers will last longer if you place the stems in deep, warm water and add a drop or two of lemon juice or an aspirin to the water in the vase. It is crucial to keep your rose plants weed-free.

AUGUST-SEPTEMBER	Regular maintenance now as your rose bush gets ready for a final blooming push in the fall.
OCTOBER-NOVEMBER	Stop fertilizing, but around Thanksgiving, feed your plant with an application of Sul-Po-Mag. Some pruning may be required, but be aware of the type of rose you are cutting, and remember that some roses bloom from the previous season's wood so prune lightly.
DECEMBER	Prune this month, keeping in mind the type of rose you are growing. Basic garden clean-up, especially paying attention to mulches. As soon as your rose loses most of its foliage, spray the plant, all of its parts and the soil around it with a dormant horticultural oil spray.

A NOTE ABOUT CHEMICAL USE

If you are concerned about the amount of pesticides that it may take to raise a quality rose bush, then you might consider one of the dozen or so newer varieties that are resistant to most rose disorders. These new creations require very little care, and seem to thrive in many difficult conditions. Though growing some of the hybrids may call for diligent pest control, there are many roses which can be raised with simple fertilization and little else. A visit to your local Extension Service office or Arboretum will reveal many of these excellent newer plants.

Rosa banksiae

Lady banks rose

'*Lutea*'   The yellow variety of this famous species, and the one that has made our coastal area famous for early spring rose cultivation. No fragrance, but lots of double yellow flowers.

In its natural state, Lady Banks is white and highly fragrant, but this species rose is not popular as a cultivated variety. We more often see the yellow version '*Lutea*'. This variety is a vigorous climber, showing massive blooming potential in early spring. It's a show-stopper, and in a good year, without a late freeze, you can expect a full specimen to cover a wall or trellis with plenty of flowers. Grow it against a wall for protection, give it good support, and prune it immediately after blooming. If it grows too much, you can clip it back during the summer, but too much cutting will diminish next year's show.

Too much shade harms blooming; otherwise any location is good, but always put this one where the crowd will see it. Over the years, it will bring lots of spring pleasure to your home garden and will make your place the envy of the neighborhood!

MONTH-BY-MONTH GUIDE FOR LADY BANKS ROSE

JANUARY	Dormancy is obvious. Look for copper-colored leaves that have remained during the winter. Most of the foliage, however, is long gone.
MARCH-APRIL	You won't need to fertilize as your Lady Banks pushes some new foliage and flower buds which may open at any time. Late this period, the whole plant will erupt into bloom.
MAY	Some flowers persist, but new growth is obvious, with long, pale green stems and small , light green foliage. Several feet of new growth is common.
JUNE	Before the fifteenth, prune selected parts of the plant.
JULY	New growth continues. Help it along with additions to your support or strengthening the arbor.
AUGUST	Continue to monitor growth and prune as needed, but do so lightly.
LABOR DAY	Feed the plant with a cup of Sul-Po-Mag, applied around the base of the plant and worked into the soil.
OCTOBER-NOVEMBER	Growth has slowed and some leaves begin to fall.
DECEMBER	Dormancy arrives as most leaves have fallen. Now is a good time to check the supports and ties.

Spirea x vanhoutte

Vanhoutte's spirea

We have chosen this hybrid spirea from the thousands of cultivated varieties within a genus that contains a hundred or more species because of its immense popularity, broad landscape usage, and simply because this spirea is just plain tough! If you live in a crowded suburban setting, along a city street or if you share a common area with neighbors this plant is for you. Vanhoutte's will grow quickly to eight feet from a clump of slender, arching branches with grey-green, small, oval leaves and plenty of vigor.

One of the most common spireas grown, this old favorite requires little care, not much pruning and provides a very nice cluster in the ornamental flower bed. Or use it as a hedge material or grouped in a shrub border. The plant is deciduous, but foliates rapidly in the spring just before it sports clusters of small, flat, ray-like flowers along the branches. This profusion of white blossoms in early spring is a delightful reminder that actual spring is just weeks away.

Healthy soil is best, slightly acidic and well-drained, and be sure you have plenty of sunlight; otherwise your Vanhoutte's will have lush growth but few flowers. This spirea will grow to eight feet with spreading arches of foliage to about four feet.

MONTH-BY-MONTH GUIDE FOR VANHOUTTE'S SPIREA

JANUARY	Though dormant, your plant may have some pale green leaves along the branches.
FEBRUARY	Protect the plant from freezing weather with good mulch and a light cover if severe temperatures threaten.
MARCH	Around the tenth of the month, fertilize your plant with a light application of 6-6-12 and apply some fresh mulch. Make sure you have watered each week for one inch accumulation.
APRIL	Blooms may appear any time as the plant shows healthy amounts of foliage.
MAY	Blooms disappear quickly, and the plant shows lots of aggressive growth.
JUNE	As soon as growth slows, prune or shape as needed, but be careful not to destroy the natural shape and structure of the arches.
JULY-SEPTEMBER	Keep your plant well-watered and replace any older mulch. Fertilize around Labor Day with a handful of superphosphate. The "dog days" of summer may cause some fungal problems, so keep the basic garden fungicides handy.
OCTOBER-NOVEMBER	Cooler days and nights bring a change of color to the foliage. Green leaves give way to some copper, bronze or purple foliage. Do not fertilize or cultivate around the base of the plant.
DECEMBER	Your spirea goes into deep dormancy now as the leaves fall and the plant shows little signs of vitality in the winter garden.

Taxodium distcihum

Bald cypress, Southern cypress, Pond cypress, Baldcypress, Swamp cypress

A drive around Wilmington's Greenfield Lake, a tour through the famous Orton Plantation or a visit to the woodland preserves in coastal Carolina will show you all the examples, great and small, that this wonderful tree has to offer. Called the "wood eternal" because of its solid heartwood, this tree has been used for furniture, heavy construction (including docks and wharves), interior trim and general millwork. But it is listed here as an ornamental because of its magnificent beauty and because it is so easy to establish. All you need is very acidic soil that is either wet or heavily compacted. A marshy wetland is perfect.

It's a conifer, but it is deciduous, so in the fall the feather-like foliage turns to a rich brown color and falls away from the tree leaving a stark, widely-branched tree along the winter skyline. The cones are hard, gray-green balls that remain on the tree or fall to the ground in autumn. The tree will reach 120 feet at maturity with a narrow, pyramid-shaped crown at the top of the branchless trunk.

This Southern classic is as much a part of our culture as grits and Faulkner, and if you have room for a massive specimen, plant this one so future generations will stand in awe of its wonderful, romantic beauty.

MONTH-BY-MONTH GUIDE FOR BALDCYPRESS

JANUARY-FEBRUARY	Multi-branched at the top of the crown and totally bare in appearance, the tree stands tall against the winter skyline. A few feathery leaves continue to drift down on windy days.
MARCH-APRIL	Tiny green leaves form along the branches as the tree foliates. Keep the water level in the pond as high as can be, and acid soil is essential; otherwise, the leaves will turn yellow.
MAY	Full foliage now as the tree moves into spring. Some cones may appear as the leaves develop into uniform, feather-like needles. The soft, slender stems are very flexible, waving in the breezes.
JUNE-SEPTEMBER	The season for bald cypress. Mature trees have large, tapered buttress flares, the roots forming "knees" which protrude from the ground as much as four or six feet.
OCTOBER-NOVEMBER	Leaves turn brown and begin to fall. No need to rake them as they break down over the winter months to form an excellent mulch. Cones may split and fall to the ground.
DECEMBER	Dormancy arrives. Wildlife will use the tree for nests and habitats.

Ternstroemia gemnenthera

Cleyera

Though this wonderful Oriental native is most often grown as a shrub, it makes an excellent addition to the natural areas of gardens when allowed to grow to full height. As a tree, it will reach forty feet with a multibranched spreading canopy of fifteen feet or more.

Often sold as Japanese cleyera (*Cleyera japonica*), this evergreen has very dark, deep green leaves in groups of four or five at the ends of slender branches. It's an evergreen, so it retains excellent color and foliage during the dormant months when other trees in the landscape have defoliated. It has the advantages of pest-free growth, no fertilization requirements and very little maintenance, though some pruning in the dormant season will preserve good shape and check unwanted growth. Flowers appear in late spring, and though they last only a short time, they are slightly fragrant and bloom at a time when other flowering trees have finished for the season. The fruit is a cluster of yellow or red berries during the late summer and fall.

Grow your cleyera in slightly acid soil with good sunlight, though the tree will tolerate some partial shade. Water is essential for best growth, so during the growing season, make sure the tree has all it needs, up to an inch weekly. Cleyeras can be pruned during the winter to nearly any height, so they are ideal for small gardens or areas where a small shade tree with dark green foliage is needed. This long-lived small tree is ideal for the coastal area, and since it is not popular as a tree, it will give your landscape a specimen that your neighbors may not have. Reliable and durable, the color of the leaves and the slender canopy make this an excellent choice for the ornamental garden or natural area.

MONTH-BY-MONTH GUIDE FOR CLEYERA

JANUARY-FEBRUARY	The tree is dormant. Some foliage may be orange or copper-colored during the winter months.
MARCH-APRIL	Some very pale foliage may appear in the whorls of previous season's growth. Late freezes may nip this new growth, but it will quickly revive. Late in the period, full growth is underway.
MAY	Flowers appear as creamy-white or yellow clusters of small florets with some fragrance. They won't last long, but new growth is obvious during the bloom cycle. New, pale green leaves "harden" rapidly and change color to rich, dark green as the summer progresses.
JUNE-AUGUST	You can prune some during this period to check unwanted growth or to maintain good balance. Test the soil and amend accordingly to maintain a pH of 5 or 6. Pale, thin foliage, or leaves with a copper-colored cast indicate a pH imbalance. You can fertilize during this period with a cup or two of tankage around the drip line, and make sure the tree is watered well.
SEPTEMBER-NOVEMBER	No more pruning now as the fall approaches, and though the tree is evergreen, some slight leaf loss is apparent and a change of color in some leaves is normal.
DECEMBER	A few branches can be harvested for indoor use as long-lasting holiday foliage.

Vaccinium ashei

Rabbiteye blueberry

Alice B. Russell

Blueberries may be America's most popular homegrown fruit because the genus contains over 150 species which are common from the Arctic Circle to the tropics. *V.ashei*, often listed as *V. corymbosum* is quite popular here along the coast, and is called rabbiteye blueberry because of the deep orange circle and dot at the top of the fruit where it breaks from the pedicel.

The species has a number of cultivated varieties, all of which perform well in the heat and humidity of the coastal area, and all of which make excellent hedges. So you'll want to plant several in a row or group. This will not only help with pollination, so you'll be able to enjoy the fruit, but will create the type of appearance these plants are famous for.

It's a spreading shrub with oval leaves which turn a brilliant yellow and red color in the fall. Small, pinkish flowers come in late spring, followed by the blueberries which last from early July into August. Birds and wildlife enjoy them as much as we do, of course, so you may need to protect the plants with some netting if you value the fruit.

Sunny locations are best. Slightly moist, acid soil is a requirement, and you'll need to check the pH every year to make sure it is below 5.0. Use garden sulfur to change the pH and you'll probably have to keep your rabbiteyes separate from other plants in the garden because of the acid requirement. Annual composting around the plant is a good way to keep the soil conditioned, but be sure not to work around the root systems because of the upper surface structure of the roots.

Alice B. Russell

Blueberries make a wonderful addition to the garden and an excellent choice for children's projects. You can expect eight feet of top growth and a spread of four feet if the plant is allowed to grow unpruned.

MONTH-BY-MONTH GUIDE FOR RABBITEYE BLUEBERRY

JANUARY	If you have not done so, prune your dormant plant this month. The berries you'll enjoy next spring are produced on last summer's growth, so don't cut too much of the plant.
FEBRUARY	Mulch around the base of the plant with several gallons of fresh compost. On the fifteenth of the month, spray the entire plant with a dormant horticultural oil spray.
MARCH	Check the soil pH. Blueberries grow best in acid soil, below 5.0. Amend the soil accordingly. Fertilize the plant with 6-6-12 fertilizer at the rate of one-quarter cup per foot of height, and add one-quarter cup of superphosphate around the base of each plant.
APRIL	New growth continues along the branches, and some flowering takes place early in the month. Look for small, pinkish-colored cup-shaped flowers. After blooming, notice some very small fruits.
MAY-JUNE	Water is essential. Watch your plant for signs of insects. Use an organic spray if needed.
JULY	Fruiting is obvious, harvest at will. Protect the shrub with bird netting.
AUGUST	Some growth continues as the fruit is harvested. You can prune parts of the plant at any time, but avoid excessive pruning.
SEPTEMBER	Late in the month, you will notice some leaf color change as the plant begins dormancy. Rich reds and yellows become obvious and some leaf loss takes place.
OCTOBER-NOVEMBER	Fall color change takes place and your plant goes into dormancy for the winter.

Viburnum tinus   (*Laurustinus*)

Laurustinus

'Gwenillian'   A nice variety that flowers and fruits from a thick shrub. Pink flowers in late winter and early spring.

'Eve Price'   An excellent cultivar for the coastal South, this deep-green, compact shrub prunes easily and will become an excellent specimen or hedge. Not very pleasant to smell, the flat, pinkish flowers are borne in winter and spring and produce remarkable blue berries.

Viburnums have become extremely popular as landscape items in the coastal area of North Carolina in the last several years. Though several hundred species and at least that many cultivated varieties are available, we have concentrated our efforts on just one, the elegant laurustinus. Some viburnums have large flowers in spring, like the famous Japanese snowball while others produce very fine, delicate, lacy flowers like the well-known doublefile viburnum. But the *tinus* species has the advantage of interesting flowers as well as deep blue berries which make the genus so attractive. On balmy days in mid-winter, it is not uncommon to see the laurustinus blossom openly with pinkish-white, large, flat flowers. Later in the season, the berries are formed which usually last well into winter. The foliage is lush and green with a silvery back and the plant is very cold hardy. Laurustinus rarely needs feeding and is virtually pest-free. The occasional caterpillar can be easily controlled with Dipel and there are no serious diseases that affect the plant. Prune in early spring, if needed, as the new growth develops, and once your plant is established try not to move it as the root system is far reaching just under the surface. Demand for this plant is not high. This can often cause difficulty in finding it as a line stock item in nurseries. But it is worth the wait and will provide you with years of maintenance-free, exceptionally strong growth. Plant yours in a partially shaded site. Well-drained soil is a must. A healthy plant will exceed ten feet of growth with a mounded spread of several feet.

MONTH-BY-MONTH GUIDE FOR LAURUSTINUS

JANUARY	It's not uncommon to see some flowers late in the month.
FEBRUARY	Blooming slowly takes place. Balmy days will produce large, pinkish-white flowers with many tiny florets. The fragrance is not very pleasant but the flowers are attractive.
MARCH	Blooming continues throughout the month, and some new growth takes place. Deep pruning will interfere with fruiting, so it is best to allow your plant to grow at will for the season.
APRIL-MAY	Water is essential as the plant grows. Some light shearing is okay, but deep pruning is not advised.
JUNE-AUGUST	Watch for caterpillars and keep your plants well-watered. Late in the period, fertilize with a light application of tankage, or one cup of bloodmeal.
SEPTEMBER	Your plant is dormant.
OCTOBER-DECEMBER	As your plant breaks dormancy just before Thanksgiving, fertilize with one-fourth cup of superphosphate

Weigela florida

Weigela

Newcomers to Southern gardening often disregard this plant because the blooming season is short, the plant occupies a large space and many homeowners make the mistake of pruning it at the wrong time to curb its growth, thus missing the wonderful flower display. But old-timers know the advantages of this classic old South beauty, and today there is a definite revival of this fully-hardy, dramatic ornamental. From a stark shrub in winter, it foliates quickly in the spring, shows vigorous growth as it flowers, often covering the entire plant with funnel-shaped, deep pink flowers which fade to light pink and white in the centers. It can attain heights and widths of eight feet or more, and requires very little care, though pruning is essential each year to encourage vigorous blooming. Grow your weigela in rich soil, a sunny location and keep it well-watered for years of healthy growth and wonderful color display in the spring.

The species plant, *W. florida*, has been cultivated for many years, and there are several varieties, all of which are excellent for our area. A well-experienced nurseryman will have a good selection including the new variegated, slightly fragrant types.

Pay close attention to the pruning dates, and keep the plant in an open, bright location with good air circulation so that you will avoid the fungal disorders that come during the late days of summer.

MONTH-BY-MONTH GUIDE FOR WEIGELA

JANUARY	Though you will lose some flowers if you prune now, it is still a good time to reach deep into the center of your plant and remove any old, scraggly branches that crowd the center, inhibiting sunlight and good air circulation. On the last day of the month, apply a cup of superphosphate around the drip line, and scratch it into the soil.
FEBRUARY-MARCH	Protect your plant from freezes and winter winds. Replace the mulch, and during the warm, windy periods of mid-to-late-March, make sure your plant is well-watered.
APRIL	Foliage appears now and the flower buds show up in the terminals and along the branches. Growth may be vigorous, up to several inches per branch, and flowering begins.
MAY	Your plant will bloom with intensity, but the flowers may not last more than a week or so.
JUNE	Prune this month only. Be careful and selective, remembering that pruning now will preserve flowers for next year, but after June fifteenth, you'll destroy bloom potential.
JULY	Water is essential. After the fifteenth, fertilize your plant with a cup of 5-10-10 premium fertilizer and a cup of Greensand.
AUGUST-OCTOBER	The "dog days" may bring some fungal disorders. If so, a light application of commercial fungicides may be needed on a cool day. Water from the ground up only, and avoid pruning.
NOVEMBER-DECEMBER	Leaves are lost as the dormant season arrives, and your plant will sleep through the winter. Replace the mulch, and water your plant deeply before Christmas.

A HANDFUL OF PERENNIALS

Perennials add a continuing show of color to the garden to compliment your ornamentals. Although their blooms may last only ten days to two weeks, if you plant with a variety of bloom-times in mind you can have a spot of color in your garden all season long. Perennials will generally live for several years — some are sturdy enough to rely on almost indefinitely. Most perennials will increase in size if you plant them in a location that suits them. They can be divided to make new plants for your garden or to give away to friends. They are definitely worth a try.

Achillea sp.

Yarrow, achillea

One of my favorite perennial plants is this prolific bloomer that seems to thrive in just about any condition. It tolerates everything we have in our coastal environment, especially heat, open sunshine and erratic rainfall. But if it has the least bit of care, this spreading plant will give you a full season of colorful, durable flowers that have some wonderful characteristics.

The foliage is usually aromatic with a spicy fragrance, and the flowers form quickly in the early summer. From then 'til fall, they'll keep coming as the plants grow steadily.

Growth habit is perfect for the perennial color garden. The feather-like foliage forms a dense clump which sends a stem up with the flat, clustered blooms. These stems reach eighteen inches in some cases, but if the plants are grown in mixed perennial beds, the stems can be less tall. The clumps spread over the garden as the summer moves along, and can be invasive.

In the old days, yarrow was found as a mustard-colored flower that was used as a dried flower as well as fresh cutting material. Over the years, we have seen some dramatic hybrids come along. 'Crimson Beauty' is a cultivar of A. *millefolium*, as is 'Cerise Queen'. The species A. *filipendulina* offers the hybrid 'Coronation Gold', and 'Moonshine' is a cross within the genus that has wonderful silvery foliage that resembles Dusty Miller.

Yarrow is a staple in the coastal garden. Don't be misled by folks who say the plant can't take the heat and humidity of the coastal area. The newer selections have eliminated many of the problems we used to face in raising this delightful, fragrant, long-lasting perennial.

MONTH-BY-MONTH GUIDE FOR YARROW

JANUARY-MARCH	The plants are dormant. Use this time to repair the perennial flower bed, clearing debris and replacing the old mulch with fresh, dry material.
APRIL	You will notice some signs of life, as more of the feathery foliage appears in the garden.
MAY-JUNE	The foliage grows rapidly and flower stems are not too far behind. Yarrow thrives in poor soil, but keep the plants watered, never letting them wilt. Broadcast a handful or two of 5-10-10 fertilizer around the flower bed before the plants get too big. Flowers can appear anytime.
JULY-SEPTEMBER	This is peak blooming time for yarrow. Keep the beds weed-free and well-watered. You will not need any pesticides or fertilizers, but if you notice any fungal diseases, open the beds for more air circulation and increased sunshine.
OCTOBER-NOVEMBER	As fall approaches, the season comes to an end for blooming, but the plants continue to grow. Dormancy is near, and growth will slow as the days get shorter and cooler.
DECEMBER	As soon as the first frost or freeze kills back the plant's top growth, replace the mulch, clean the beds and remove any debris from the garden. Normally, unless the winter is very severe, some delicate basal leaves will persist just above the ground. You can move your yarrow to another location or divide the clumps now.

Canna x generalis

Garden canna

These striking plants are well known in coastal Carolina, and are very popular in just about any landscape plan. We see them used along the right-of-ways in highway plantings, in the medians of Interstate highways, commercial sites and all sorts of residential flower beds. Big and showy, cannas are old summer favorites for good reason. They don't require much care, they are are offered in a wide variety of colors and growth habits and will spread over the perennial garden.

If you are used to raising cannas in other parts of the country, you probably had to dig them each fall and store them for the winter, or replant them in the spring from new rootstock. But here in the coastal Carolinas, we are able to keep our cannas in the ground year after year, and unless we have a severe winter, they survive very well.

Garden cannas come in a number of colors, so choose them to suit your color scheme. Some cultivars have variegated foliage, but all cannas bloom from tall stalks, some as high as four feet, topped with three or four blossoms which open at various times. The blooms last for several days, but the plants will throw flowers over several months, and if you plant several types, you'll have color from early spring to fall.

In general they are pest-free; however they are sometimes bothered by caterpillars that roll the leaves. A dusting of DE as the foliage matures will prevent pests.

Keep the soil moist, do not let the plants dry out and provide plenty of sunshine.

Raising cannas can be a lot of fun, especially if you mix the colors. Reliable and vibrant, they'll offer good color and texture to the perennial flower garden.

MONTH-BY-MONTH GUIDE FOR CANNA

JANUARY-MARCH	The tuberous roots are dormant. You can transplant now if you want.
APRIL	Clean the flower bed, replace the mulch and water the cannas before they appear. By late this month, you'll see some activity as they break ground. Fertilize them with a handful of 5-10-10 fertilizer. To prevent snails and slugs or caterpillars from attacking the plants, scatter a handful of DE around the bases of the plants as they emerge.
MAY-JUNE	Give your cannas plenty of room to grow. Stake the plants' stalks if they need the support.
JULY-SEPTEMBER	Water is essential. The roots are close to the surface, so you might have to water daily. Reapply the DE if you notice pests. In early August, apply another dose of 5-10-10. Keep the mulch clean and dry on the surface.
OCTOBER-NOVEMBER	As the blooms fade and fall approaches, allow the stalks to remain. Maintain watering and a weed-free, clean flower bed.
DECEMBER	The first frost or freeze will kill the plants back to the ground. Collect all the old stalks, leaves and other debris. Replace the mulch and transplant the roots this month.

Chrysanthemum maximum

Shasta daisy

The daisy is perhaps America's most recognized flower, and here along the coast of the Carolinas, it can be found in many forms. It's a member of a large family, but the shasta is perhaps the daisy most folks want in the perennial garden. It's tall and vigorous, blooms for a long period in the summer garden, and provides a fresh, cool appearance on a hot summer day.

C. maximum is a large plant, producing flowers that are two feet tall and over an inch across. The foliage is not very interesting, and like most perennial plants, is coarse. But the stems produce single flower heads of white blossoms with lots of petals and green centers. Some varieties make double flowers, but all are white.

The plants prefer open sunshine, well-drained soil and moist, fertile conditions. You'll need to feed the plants a few times during the growing season.

'Alaska' is an excellent cultivar which has very large, flat-faced flowers and 'Little Miss Muffet' is a semi-double flower. The species *C. superbum* is synonymous with *C. maximum*, and a plant formerly listed as *C. superbum* called 'Elizabeth' is an old favorite in the Southern garden.

MONTH-BY-MONTH GUIDE FOR SHASTA DAISY

JANUARY-MARCH	The dormant plant will normally retain a few basal leaves as it waits for warmer weather to renew its growth cycle.
APRIL	At the first signs of spring break, you'll see more foliage appear around the bases of the plants. Water them well, and scatter a handful or two of 5-10-10 fertilizer around the flower bed. Replace the mulch with fresh material, and eliminate any weeds.
MAY-JUNE	You'll need to water the plants regularly as they grow, especially when the flower heads are forming. To keep lace bugs and beetles from nibbling the leaves and flowers, apply some DE if you have a problem.
JULY-SEPTEMBER	Around the fourth of July fertilize the plants just as you did in the spring. Flowers are forming regularly now as summer progresses. Water is essential. Keep the flower bed weed-free. Pick flowers often to encourage more blooming.
OCTOBER-NOVEMBER	Most flowering is complete. Keep the flower bed clean and weed-free. Though blooming may stop, the plants are still active, so maintain normal care.
DECEMBER	The plants have faded during the fall, and the first frost or freeze will kill back the plant's top growth. However, unless the winter is unusually severe, some basil leaves will continue to show themselves close to the ground throughout the cold season.

Clematis paniculata

Sweet autumn clematis

Alice B. Russell

Alice B. Russell

There are over two hundred species of clematis and perhaps that many cultivated varieties of this wonderful vine, some of which rival any trailing ornamental for floral display, foliage and coverage. But we have chosen this one species, C. *paniculata*, for your pleasure because it has been appreciated by so many coastal Carolina gardeners for many years. It symbolizes the graceful, fragrant beauty of the South in late summer, when lazy days, cool sunsets and light breezes accentuate the effect of this rambler.

It has become part of the wild landscape in many rural areas, though in cultivation it is very effective. Quickly running over fences, up tree stumps, over walls and around obstacles, it grows rapidly, scrambling into sunlight through the thickest hedges and shrubs. It will spend the entire summer growing, becoming a massive vining ornamental, and by the time late summer arrives, it will be ready to bloom. And bloom it will! Masses of white fragrant flowers form distinctive seed pods which cover the vine from August through September.

The plant is somewhat difficult to grow, as all clematis are. But once established, it will become a featured part of your summer garden even though you'll have to cultivate it. Grow this spectacular vine in rich, cool, well-drained soil. It is essential not to let the plant dry out during the growing season. Though sunlight is not a concern for the vine itself, it will have to be able to reach sunlight as it grows in order to bloom. Choose a spot that will provide some support. A trellis, tree stump, fence, string supports up the side of the house, or even existing hedges all make fine supports. It will bloom on current wood, so prune it in the winter after it loses its leaves. Mulch it well, and make sure you protect it from late freezes by cutting it back. Prune it to only twelve or more inches tall.

You may have some trouble finding it in the nursery, but it is certainly worth the effort. In the past it has been sold by the common name, as well as C. *maximowicziana*.

If it's clematis you want, then consider this late-summer perennial, one that will delight your friends and family with its fragrance and amazing growth habit.

194

MONTH-BY-MONTH GUIDE FOR SWEET AUTUMN CLEMATIS

JANUARY-MARCH	Not much is left of this once strident plant as dormancy sets in, and the vine has completely faded. Find the old runners and prune them back to the desired height, though no more than twelve or sixteen inches above ground. Late freezes may harm the plant. Plenty of mulch will help the roots stay protected.
APRIL	Water the plant well during dry periods, and apply a cup of 5-10-10 fertilizer and one-half cup of superphosphate around the base of the plant. Growth may appear anytime.
MAY-JUNE	Test the soil pH. Your vine will grow best in neutral soil, so add lime now as needed. Water is essential. If the vine does not cling to the support, help it along so it will be able to reach the sunlight.
JULY	It is not uncommon to see some flowers along the sunny side of the branches. Water at half an inch every three days. If you notice snails and slugs, treat the plant with DE.
AUGUST	Blooming can take place anytime. No more care is required.
SEPTEMBER-OCTOBER	Blooming may continue. Seed heads form where flowers once appeared. Do not prune.
NOVEMBER	Dormancy slows blooming, and by Thanksgiving, the plant begins to lose some foliage.
DECEMBER	Rapidly losing its leaves, the vine slips into dormancy. It's a good time to repair the support, extend it or modify it for next year's growth.

Coreopsis lanceolata

Coreopsis

Any coastal resident who is flower-conscious will recognize this little early summer blooming flower. The foliage is nondescript, but the flowers are bright yellow daisy-like blossoms that have a golden eye. They are abundant in the meadows and fields of the coastal area, and they are frequently sold in the perennial flower shops for use in home gardens.

Since they are cultivated flowers from wild selections, they tend to do better when they are treated less formally. Use them in meadow plantings or open areas as opposed to structured settings. *C. lanceolata* grows to no more than a foot or so in height and blooms for several months. The plant is short-lived, but it reseeds it self generously, so once planted, you'll have a steady supply. The plants may even become invasive. Open sunshine is best, and this tough little plant will tolerate heat and drought.

There are a number of cultivars available. 'Early Sunrise' is an All-America Selection Winner. 'Baby Sun' is an excellent tall grower and 'Sunray' produces a double flower from a stem that reaches two feet in height.

The species gets confused with *C. auriculata* and *C. verticillata*, both of which are native wildflowers. The tell-tags in the nursery will describe which plant you are purchasing, but *C. lanceolata* is regarded as the best species for the coastal area.

MONTH-BY-MONTH GUIDE FOR COREOPSIS

JANUARY-MARCH	You can dig some clumps of coreopsis and transplant them this month if you know where they are planted.
APRIL	A light application of 5-10-10 fertilizer broadcast over the flower bed is all your coreopsis will need for the entire season. Water the plants as they appear in the garden.
MAY-JUNE	Keep the flower bed weed-free, but do not disturb the plants. A light application of mulch is an excellent idea this month.
JULY-AUGUST	The plants will bloom this period. If you want them to reseed themselves, then allow the plants to go untended. If you "deadhead" the plants by picking the spent blossoms, you'll encourage more blooming. Several flowers will appear from the same plant, and it will spread during the growing season. Keep the plants watered as the bloom.
SEPTEMBER-OCTOBER	Most blooming has stopped in the heat of the summer, but the plants will continue to grow. Keep them weed-free, but do not fertilize. Pests will not be a problem.
NOVEMBER	Before dormancy sets in, tag the plants so you'll know where they are planted.
DECEMBER	The first frost or freeze will kill the tops of the plants.

Dianthus caryophyllus

Carnation, pinks

The name "pinks" is old-fashioned and comes from the days when this wonderful, early spring flower covered small areas of the garden or lawn just before the end of May. One of the first perennials to show color in the spring, it is a delightful ground cover, and will spread rapidly after it blooms. You can expect the plant to repeat for many years, and it seems to thrive on little care.

Six or eight inches tall is all it gets, but it spreads over several feet in a growing season. You can dig sections of the ground in which the plant grows just about anytime, but it's best to transplant these little carnations in early summer before they go into dormancy.

In mild winters, the foliage may appear early and stay around 'til spring when the flowers bloom.

Alkaline soil is best, so a soil test is a good idea in the fall. Don't mulch too heavily. There are quite a few cultivated varieties, but the old-fashioned species plant is excellent.

This plant is sometimes confused with *D. plumarius,* the familiar "grass pinks" of the Piedmont.

Alice B. Russell

MONTH-BY-MONTH GUIDE FOR PINKS

JANUARY-FEBRUARY	Though your plant is dormant, its steely-green foliage may appear, spreading itself around the garden.
MARCH	Using a water-soluble fertilizer which has been enhanced with the "Dr. Plant's Formula," spray the mats of foliage every ten days or so beginning on the fifteenth of the month. If you notice any weeds, be sure to clip them back or remove them without disturbing the pinks.
APRIL	Around the fifteenth of the month, the plants will begin to show growth. Get ready for blooming which is just a few weeks away. Repeat the fertilizer application once more.
MAY	The mats of foliage will bloom anytime now with a cloud of pink, carnation-like flowers. You can prune the plants back as soon as they finish blooming. As soon as they finish blooming, you can divide the plants.
JUNE-AUGUST	The heat of the summer will send the plants into dormancy. You may not notice any sign of them during the next few months.
SEPTEMBER-OCTOBER	The foliage of the plants may reappear. Do nothing to disturb them. Have the soil tested and amend accordingly for neutral pH.
NOVEMBER	You can divide the plants now if you didn't do it in the spring.
DECEMBER	Some foliage may persist during the colder months, but a frost or freeze might eliminate the visible parts of the plant.

Alice B. Russell

Digitalis purpurea

Foxglove

!ALL PARTS OF THIS PLANT ARE POISONOUS!

Foxgloves are actually biennials, in that they bloom the second year of their life spans and then die. It gets a little confusing dealing with these plants, because you will usually be purchasing plants that are one-year-old already, and thus are ready to bloom the spring and summer that you plant them. However, because of their biennial nature they will not return the following year.

What makes foxgloves last in the perennial garden is their ability to seed themselves. So after a year or so of growing these plants, and allowing them to seed, you should have a good clump which will continue on indefinitely..

They grow from clumps of thick, fleshy basal leaves which last during the winter months in the garden. In early spring they produce a spike from the center of the plant that grows to sixteen inches tall, bearing bell-shaped flowers which can be multi-colored, peach, cream or purple. Though not fragrant, these flowers attract birds and butterflies and last for several weeks. The plant will throw only one flower spike per season, but the foliage will persist for awhile longer.

Foxglove is a fine Southern plant, either as part of the mixed color garden, along a fence or toward the back or center of a flower bed. There are several named cultivars, but if you purchase ordinary foxglove in the perennial nursery, you'll have a carefree plant that performs well in the heat of the summer.

Alice B. Russell

MONTH-BY-MONTH GUIDE FOR FOXGLOVE

JANUARY-MARCH	It's not uncommon to have the clumps of basal leaves persist during the milder winters. Do not disturb them.
APRIL	Toward the end of the month, the flower spike may begin to grow from the center of the plant. Look for activity in the center of the plant. Apply a general broadcast of 5-10-10 premium fertilizer over the entire flower bed, or around the base of your plants. Water is essential, so make sure the bed or the plants get at least half an inch every three days.
MAY-JUNE	The plant may bloom. Flowers start along the length of the spike, opening from the bottom up, the top blooms opening a week or so after the bottom flowers. Allow the seeds to form and drop. Do not harvest the spike.
JULY	Flowering may continue from some plants. Clumps that are forming in the first year will not produce a flower.
AUGUST	Though pests will not be a usual problem, you might notice some slugs and snails in the foxgloves. Use DE to treat them.
SEPTEMBER-OCTOBER	The season is over for blooming, but much is going on in the root systems of the plants. Do not disturb the plants. Do not fertilize, but make sure you water regularly.
NOVEMBER-DECEMBER	The spikes have disappeared and the plant begins to wane. Though it may not entirely die back, dormancy is obvious.

Eupatorium coelestinum

Mist flower, ageratum

In the late summer, when most other perennials have set seed and are fading, you will find this vigorous plant in full bloom. It spends most of the summer forming a large mound of foliage, and then produces clouds of dark blue flowers which last for weeks into the fall.

As it grows during the summer, you'll have to check the spread so that it doesn't invade other parts of the flower bed; otherwise, it will form a mound of five or six feet in a single season. The flowers are borne on simple stalks above the foliage, reaching several feet. It's a sturdy plant, but tends to ramble a bit, so you may need to support some of the weaker plants.

Though it is originally a cultivated plant, mist flower has out-run the garden and now appears all over the area, in ditch banks, abandoned fields and old homesites. But despite its weediness, it makes a delightful summer perennial, and because it is one of the few true-blue flowers in the perennial garden, it is worth the effort to cultivate it. Mist flower is the hardy version of annual ageratum.

Keep the beds weed-free, the soil well-drained and don't overfertilize the plants. As it blooms, grab a handful every day or two for cut flowers.

MONTH-BY-MONTH GUIDE FOR MIST FLOWER

JANUARY-MARCH	The plants die back during the winter, and there is little sign of them during the late winter. Rake the beds and replace the mulch.
APRIL	As spring approaches, you may see some signs of the plants coming to life. Mark the bed, and add some compost to the flower bed. Water the plants, and scatter or broadcast a handful or two of 5-10-10 fertilizer.
MAY-JUNE	Keep the bed weed-free. Don't allow the plants to stand in water. As they grow, prune them away from other parts of the bed if they become invasive. Add mulch or compost as needed. Water is essential, but make sure the soil is well-drained.
JULY-AUGUST	Flowering approaches. The plants will continue to grow and expand. Flower heads will appear.
SEPTEMBER-OCTOBER	Flowering becomes obvious as the cooler days come in. Mist flower spikes are short stems above the clumps of foliage and will bear plenty of flat, feathery blossoms. Do not disturb the plants as they bloom.
NOVEMBER	As blooming ceases, the plants become dormant. The foliage will pale to a yellow color, then drop away from the plants. Now is a good time to clean up the flower bed a bit, but avoid cultivating around the roots of your mist flower plants.
DECEMBER	Dormancy is obvious, and after the first freeze, your plants will disappear. Rake away dead material and mulch the perennial garden.

Hedychium coronarium

Ginger lily

There is no fragrance in the perennial flower garden quite like ginger lilies. That is probably what has made them so popular over the years as coastal perennials. But the flower is rather showy itself. Produced on four- or five-foot stalks that have coarse, long, pale green leaves, the blossoms are produced from a pod-like structure with white petals and prominent stamens.

The plant is not a true lily because it grows from a fibrous root which spreads easily through the garden. It can be divided in the dormant season quite readily, and will bloom in the first year after dividing.

Grow your ginger lily in partial sun or shade and moist, rich soil. Maintain a slightly acid pH, but if you compost the plants every year, you'll keep a healthy, balanced soil. Don't overfertilize these plants.

Once a very popular late-summer perennial, ginger lilies have fallen into disfavor in the last twenty-five years. Today, they are becoming more popular as coastal gardeners have returned to the classic perennials that were once so much a part of nearly every home garden. You may have to look a little harder to find them in the stores, but once you establish them, you'll have a bed of amazing plants that are intensely fragrant and long lasting in the garden they are dramatic perennials that last for many years.

MONTH-BY-MONTH GUIDE FOR GINGER LILY

JANUARY-FEBRUARY	If you have not done so, divide the roots or transplant them anytime during this period.
MARCH	Make sure the flower bed around your ginger lilies is clean and weed-free. Any debris left from the previous season should be removed, especially older stalks and leaves. Replace the mulch with fresh material.
APRIL	As the season warms, notice some new growth from the roots of the old plants. Coarse leaves on small spikes will extend above the soil line.
MAY-JUNE	Water is essential as the stalks grow. The roots are right at the surface, so avoid working or cultivating around the plants. Keep the bed free from weeds. If insects, caterpillars or bugs become a problem, treat the plants with DE or pyrethrins.
JULY-AUGUST	Continue to water the plants, and as they reach four or five feet, you may have to support them. Notice some flower pods forming at the ends of the stalks. Toward the end of the period, some flowers may show.
SEPTEMBER	This is a prime month for ginger lilies. They will bloom vigorously, each plant producing a single stalk with a good-sized flower. The pod may contain several blossoms, each of which will open slowly. The fragrance is very noticeable. Continue to treat for insects, and ants may roam the flowers. Ginger lilies make excellent cut flowers.
OCTOBER-NOVEMBER	In our area of the South, the mild fall will encourage a slightly longer bloom period. Flowers and fragrance will persist. Some of the older plants will begin to droop and fade as fall approaches.
DECEMBER	The first freeze will kill the tops of the plants, triggering dormancy. Clean up the flower bed and remove the dead stalks and leaves. Be sure to mark the bed carefully so you will know where the ginger lilies are during the dormant season. Good garden sanitation is a must. The roots can be divided during this period.

Hemorocallis sp

Daylily

Few coastal perennials enjoy as much popularity as daylilies.Found in nearly every type of landscape plan and garden, these wonderful lily-like plants are perfect for massed beds, borders and natural settings. They create amazing color in the summer garden, they bloom for a long season and are carefree. The "fans" multiply quickly in the growing season and provide just about any color and growth habit you wish. From short, low growers to tall, arching spikes, they are featured plants along highway right-of-ways, in commercial flower beds and in residential gardens.

Quite a few daylily societies have formed active local clubs, and the collections of these wonderful plants are easy and enjoyable to start. Though some folks trade daylilies for "big bucks," you can easily purchase the old standbys for just a few dollars.

Daylilies are edible and can make delightful additions to dinner plates and salads. Some people fry new flower buds or mix them in with stir fry dishes. Each flower on a multi-flowered spike lasts for only one day, so enjoy them as much as possible for the time they bloom. Grow as many as you have room for, and be sure to select several cultivars so that you will have blooms during the entire summer season. That way, your perennial garden will never be without a colorful daylily nodding a spike or two of flowers someplace in the flower bed.

The most popular, 'Stella d'Oro', is a bright yellow, compact, vigorous grower. 'Rocket City' is a tall grower with a large, orange-yellow flower that blooms in mid-season. In mid-summer try 'Grape Ripple' for a rich, purple bloom. 'Patricia Faye' and 'Marcia Faye' are popular mid-season bloomers which offer creamy, peach-colored flowers, and the late bloomer 'Stafford' with a brilliant, red-orange flower grows tall and erect.

There are thousands from which to choose, but all of them will need plenty of sunshine, well-drained, rich soil with slightly acid pH, and a good dose of fertilizer in late spring to help them along. Plant them "up front" so your collection of daylilies will delight your neighbors and make your garden the showplace of the community.

MONTH-BY-MONTH GUIDE FOR DAYLILY

JANUARY	No sign of your plants appear as the dormant season continues and your plants survive only below ground. Do not dig around the fans or disturb the roots.
FEBRUARY	Scatter a handful of bonemeal over the soil surface near and around your hemorocallis beds.
MARCH-APRIL	Though hemorocallis are not really lilies, you might notice some lily-like foliage appearing on the soil surface. Do nothing. A late freeze may "nip" the foliage tips, but will cause no problem.
MAY-JUNE	As the foliage pops up, scatter a handful or two of tankage around the bed. Flower spikes may appear at any time, especially from the early bloomers. Look for three or four buds per stem. Flowers open in the morning and close at night, the spent blossoms falling away from the spike on the second day. Flowers will appear one at a time and will last for one day only, thus the name daylily.
JULY-AUGUST	Seed pods appear on the spent spikes, and you should allow them to stand. Slugs may feed on some flowers, and if they become a problem, apply a handful or two of DE around each plant. Japanese beetles are active now, so keep the pyrethrins handy. Do not eat flowers that have been treated. Mid-season and late blooming varieties will show color. Early bloomers have lots of seed pods. You may notice some brown leaves and dead flower spikes which cause little concern.
SEPTEMBER-OCTOBER	A late flush of flowers is possible from any variety and some some early bloomers may repeat. Enjoy the waning days of your daylilies. It's a good time to divide your plants.
NOVEMBER	The cool fall days send plants into partial dormancy. Watch as they fade away for the winter.
DECEMBER	Plants ease into dormancy as the days become shorter and colder. Clip away dead foliage and replace the mulch. Your once-vigorous hemorocallis are asleep now as winter sets in.

Hosta

Plantain lilies

Hostas, or plantain lilies as some call them, are gaining popularity across the coastal area as excellent landscape plants. They appear not only as ground covers in shady, moist places, but as specimen plants and massed groups in the newer, more compact gardens of patio homes. They do well in shaded deck containers too, and condominium home gardens. Hostas are grown for their foliage and lush display. The flowers are long-lasting and though not striking, do offer some summer color. Fully hardy, hostas will form thick clumps in just a few years. They die completely back in the winter, but are one of the first spring plants to break ground. They are long-lived, so they'll give you years of wonderful growth, and the only real pest they have is slugs, which eat the foliage. An occasional fungus gets into the stem, but beside slugs and this fungus, you'll have little trouble raising them.

There are about forty species in the genus, and from these come the two hundred or so cultivated varieties, all of which perform well in this area. None is more popular than another, but the *H. plantaginea* species is fragrant, grows with more sunshine and blooms a little later than most others.

Hosta collecting is a popular hobby. Though all of the plants are readily available, some are more prized and become featured plants in hosta enthusiasts' gardens. They can be a little expensive at purchase, but provide years of quality, perennial pleasure. Many are pure green, while some have variegated foliage. The flowers of most are light lilac in color.

MONTH-BY-MONTH GUIDE FOR HOSTA

JANUARY-FEBRUARY	Your hosta is dormant, and there is no sign from it that it even exists. Unless you have a dedicated hosta bed, you might tag the bed with some markers so that you'll know where they have been planted.
MARCH	A warm month may produce some signs of growth, but your dormant plant will remain below ground for the most part.
APRIL-MAY	As the soil temperature rises, so does the growth of your plant. Pale green leaves will push through the soil. Fertilize each plant with one-fourth cup of bloodmeal.
JUNE	Some cultivars bloom this month. Basal leaves should be well-formed and developed. Tall flower spikes well above the plant will show color. Bees are readily attracted. For snail and slug control, use DE. For Southern blight, a fungus that rots the crown, use a basic garden fungicide.
JULY-AUGUST	As soon as your plant stops blooming you can divide the clump, but it is best to complete the division before Labor Day. Keep in mind that hostas will form large clumps over the years, and the larger plants are quite attractive. Divide them only if you need the space or want to propagate.
SEPTEMBER-NOVEMBER	Enjoy the foliage of your hosta. Normal maintenance now as fall approaches. In rainy weather, consider another dose of bloodmeal or tankage to keep the plants looking their best.
DECEMBER	Cold days and nights will send your hosta below ground for the winter.

Lantana camara

Lantana

The ray-like flowers of this colorful garden perennial are perfect for borders, small pure beds of this plant or hanging baskets. When grown in containers, lantana can be used on sunny decks, on the patio or placed at various levels on the steps to the porch. It's perfect for the beach, and any sunny, well-drained garden location with ordinary soil will grow a healthy clump of lantana.

It spreads over several feet in a growing season and produces flat flowers on nodding stems that will reach a foot or so in height.

The flowers are multi-colored with rosy-hues, white, cream-colored or pink and orange. They have a bright, long-lasting appearance, and will bloom all summer. If you are familiar with lantana as an annual plant, you'll be pleased to find that here in the coastal area of the South it is treated as a perennial. As soon as it goes into dormancy, prune it back to keep the woody nature of the stems at a minimum, and with some light protection in the winter, it will return year after year. Some of the newer cultivars are dwarfs which make for low border use. Most are creamy-white; however, there are some beautiful yellow varieties.

Lantana is a strong plant that takes the summer heat and tolerates average soil and some drought. But be careful not to let the plant dry out completely.

MONTH-BY-MONTH GUIDE FOR LANTANA

JANUARY-MARCH	If you haven't pruned the plant by reducing it to a third of its summer height, do so now. Clean the bed, rake away all debris and apply fresh mulch.
APRIL	You may notice some growth from the base of the plant. Apply a handful or two of 5-10-10 premium fertilizer broadcast over the flower garden or around the plants. Water the plants well and weed the garden. Some fresh compost around the plants will keep the root system moist.
MAY-JUNE	As the plants expand, you'll notice some flower buds forming. Make sure you have enough sunshine above the plants to support good blooming. Water the plants and keep them weed-free. Blooming begins in late June.
JULY-SEPTEMBER	Flowering continues. Protect the plants from windy conditions that dry out the plant and stop its blooming. Keep the plant well-watered and weed-free.
OCTOBER-NOVEMBER	The foliage will pale as dormancy approaches. As soon as flowering stops, lightly prune the plant. After the first frost or freeze, prune the plant by reducing it to one-third its summer height and spread. Maintain good garden sanitation and watering.
DECEMBER	Replace the mulch and clean the flower bed.

Lycoris radiata

Spider lily

Dianne Birkemo, Courtesy of N.C. Botanical Garden

The exotic flower from this common bulb plant appears in early September as a surprise, because even though we have come to expect it each year, there is no indication that it is about to bloom until it suddenly appears. The flower comes on an eight- or ten-inch spike which grows quickly. The red-orange flowers have very prominent stamens and there appear to be many blossoms which circle the top of the spike. Foliage is absent until the flower fades.

This is an old-fashioned flower which was quite common at one time throughout the South, but is not seen as much these days, though it is now enjoying a revival as folks like to plant perennial plants that return year after year without a lot of care.

Spider lilies fit the bill. They are easy to grow, but a word of caution: be sure to plant them where they will remain untouched for years. Since the foliage is absent for such a long period of time, it is easy to forget that they are a part of your landscape.

On a sunny fall day, you'll be surprised to see them once again, as they return for another show when you least expect them.

MONTH-BY-MONTH GUIDE FOR SPIDER LILY

JANUARY	Some foliage persists, but for the most part, the leaves have gone.
FEBRUARY-APRIL	The remaining leaves that survived the winter are still up, but they are about to disappear.
MAY-AUGUST	There is no indication in the yard or garden that your lilies are alive. But below the surface of the soil, they are preparing to do some blooming in the fall. If you have marked the plants with tell-tags, you'll be able to watch as they appear. A handful of bonemeal applied near them in late July is beneficial, but they have most likely received all the feeding they need as you tend a summer garden and lawn that are active while the spider lilies are dormant.
SEPTEMBER	Your spider lilies will bloom. Flowers last for a week or so.
OCTOBER-DECEMBER	As the flowers fade, the strap-like leaves appear. A profusion of foliage replaces the slender, bare flower stalk. Be sure not to disturb the foliage or the plants.

Monarda didyma

Bee balm

Rob Gardner, Courtesy of N.C. Botanical Garden

This fragrant perennial is a coarse plant that bears some very colorful flowers throughout the summer. The leaves are lance-shaped and sometimes bear the signs of insect attacks. The stems that support the flowers are square and covered with stiff hairs. The plant is not very attractive.

But the flowers make up for the unsightliness of the foliage. Usually bright crimson in color, they are large blooms, almost four inches across. The bracts at the base of the bloom are deeper in color which seems to heighten the color of the flower. Shaped like a tulip, the flower has very pronounced stamens and internal parts. It is not an oddity, but it does have an exotic appearance, and the fragrance is unusual and quite appealing.

The plant is easy to grow, has only a few pests, and can be grown in a variety of soil conditions. It tolerates heat and average soil, but needs water on a regular basis to encourage good growth and blooming.

A dose of fertilizer in the early spring will supply all it needs for the season, and you can expect several months of flowers from this erect plant. It grows in sun or partial shade, spreads rapidly in the garden by underground stems, and can be invasive. North Carolina State University advises dividing it every three years, though some perennial gardeners allow it to expand at will. You can expect two feet in height and a spread of one or two feet by summer's end.

It's a native in parts of the Midwest, but here we grow a cultivated variety called 'Croftway Pink.' A deeper red flower is borne on 'Mahogany'. There are also some lighter colored varieties, and a purple flower sold to commercial cut flower dealers.

MONTH-BY-MONTH GUIDE FOR BEE BALM

JANUARY-MARCH	The flower bed needs to be clean and debris free. In the first week of March, fertilize the plants with a light application of 5-10-10 broadcast over the bed or applied around the plants. Change the mulch to fresh, dry material.
APRIL	As spring break takes place, your plant will show signs of growth. It will need a half inch of water every three days, and mulch to keep the soil moist. Never let the plant dry out.
MAY-JUNE	Keep the plants weed-free and in open sunshine with good air circulation. Mildew attacks these plants and can be eliminated by opening the growing conditions. Make sure you water regularly. If you notice fungal attacks, spray the plants with a solution of one-quarter cup baking soda, a teaspoon of dish detergent mixed in a gallon of water and a teaspoon of household ammonia every ten days. Avoid fertilizers. Flowers may show color anytime after June first.
JULY-AUGUST	The plant will continue to bloom and will grow with vigor. The heat of the summer may slow some flowering.
SEPTEMBER-NOVEMBER	Though flowering will slow, and may even stop, the plant will continue to grow. Even though it may not flower, it will still need the basic care of water, weeding and disease control. Maintenance is a must. Around Thanksgiving, apply some fresh compost around the base of the plants.
DECEMBER	You can divide the plants this month. Otherwise, good garden sanitation this month and little else will be required as the plant slips into dormancy. A frost or freeze will kill most above-ground foliage.

Rudbeckia fulgida

Blackeyed Susan

This old favorite of the Southern garden is one of the easiest plants to grow in the perennial color garden, and from mid-summer into the fall, you'll have lots of bright yellow flowers from this extremely durable plant. Keep it watered and grow it in a sunny spot, and the flowers will continue for several months.

Flowers appear on stems above clumps of dark-green foliage with two or three blooms per stem. The plant will grow to several feet tall and spread over a foot or so. The cultivar 'Goldstrum' is a popular plant, often sold as coneflower, and unlike other hybrids, it will seed itself in the garden with good reliability.

For carefree gardening and color that lasts all summer, plant this familiar garden favorite.

MONTH-BY-MONTH GUIDE FOR BLACKEYED SUSAN

JANUARY-MARCH	The plant is dormant. Good garden sanitation before the spring season approaches. Rake away old mulch and replace it with clean, dry material. Water the flower bed, and scatter a handful or two of 5-10-10 premium grade fertilizer around the plants before they appear in the early spring.
APRIL	Spring break will spark some growth from the plants. Make sure the flowers will grow in sunny spots and that they are watered regularly.
MAY-JUNE	Normal maintenance now as the plants get ready to show color. Water is essential, but the soil must be well-drained. You won't need to fertilize, but keep the weeds out and apply some mulch.
JULY-SEPTEMBER	This is the peak blooming time for Blackeyed Susans. Water is important and you can help the plants preserve moisture by making sure they are weed-free and mulched. Allow spent blossoms to stay on the plant. Avoid cultivating around the plants.
OCTOBER-NOVEMBER	As fall approaches, the plants will stop blooming and ease into dormancy. The lance-shaped foliage will die back slightly in cooler weather. Maintain watering and weeding.
DECEMBER	A light application of compost will help the plants stay healthy during the winter, and now is a good time to divide them. Clean the beds and rake away debris.

Verbena canadensis

Rose verbena

Don't be confused by the vast number of types of cultivated varieties of verbena sold in the markets today. The genus is large and contains quite a few species of perennial and annual plants, available as groundcovers and upright flowering plants. *V. canadensis* is the most popular in the coastal area because of its spreading growth habit, wonderful color (from pink to rose to deep purple) and hardiness. Rose verbena can grow tall, up to twelve inches, but it will usually stay close to the ground, running into every angle of the flower bed and rooting wherever it touches the ground. The flowers are prolific, appearing on dense mats of foliage all summer and into the fall. They are usually clusters of small, tubular blossoms that seem to thrive in just about any soil. Verbena can be invasive, almost weed-like, and is perfect for borders, massed plantings and clustered in perennial flower beds. For color and display, it's without compare, and will provide years of dynamic growth, exceptional color and and vigorous show. From early spring to fall, *Verbena canadensis* will never disappoint you, and will quickly become a favorite in the annual or perennial flower garden. Plant several colors and varieties and watch this perennial give you all the show you expect from a perennial plant.

MONTH-BY-MONTH GUIDE FOR VERBENA

JANUARY- MARCH	Your verbena is dormant. What once was a lush, dark green mat of foliage is now a mass of gray-green twigs and stems that appear weak and thin. Protect your plants in severe cold weather, as verbena will not tolerate temperatures that are too cold for too long.
APRIL-MAY	Wake up time. Foliage begins to appear and the "mat" begins to form again, much as you recall from the previous summer. If not, there's a good chance that you have lost your plant to the cold weather. As the old plant leaves out, fertilize it with a handful or two of premium 5-10-10 fertilizer applied over the entire perennial flower bed or around each plant. If you are planting for the first time, be sure not to place any fertilizer directly into the hole.
JUNE-AUGUST	Blooms appear regularly now as the season for perennials reaches its peak. Fertilize every time you water with water soluble plant food enhanced with the "Dr. Plant's Fertilizer Formula."
SEPTEMBER-DECEMBER	Blooming slows now as the season comes to a close. Your verbena is getting "sleepy." Just after Christmas, amend the flower bed with compost and fresh mulch.

Veronica spicata

Spiked speedwell

One of the earliest perennials to show color, this familiar "rat tail" produces a dark blue flower that stands above a small cluster of thin, pale foliage. It spreads during the summer, but is not invasive, and will remain confined to a small area over several years. The blooms last for a week or so, and the plant is only twelve to twenty inches tall.

It's cold hardy, but will not tolerate freezing soil, so protect it during the dormant season with an extra dose of compost and clean, dry mulch. A shot of fertilizer in the early spring will help it along, but it doesn't need a lot of cultivation.

Spiked speedwell is old-fashioned, and appears in seed catalogues from the late 1800s. A delightful addition to the garden, especially when mixed with yellow coreopsis or daylilies, you'll enjoy this small, colorful plant. The species plant is just fine for our area, though the hybrid 'Sunny Blue' is a more vibrant plant which will exceed two feet in growth. 'Icicle' is a white cultivar that is an excellent performer.

MONTH-BY-MONTH GUIDE FOR SPIKED SPEEDWELL

JANUARY-FEBRUARY	Clean the flower bed and replace the mulch. Now is a good time to move your speedwell to a sunny location or an area that offers good drainage.
MARCH	Though the plant will tolerate poor soil and drought, it's always best to water the flower bed before the plant becomes active. Spring break is near. Broadcast a handful of 5-10-10 premium grade fertilizer around the bed and among the plants. Do not overfeed.
APRIL	Keep the bed weed-free, water the plants regularly and apply some compost to the bed. Replace the mulch with clean, dry material. The plants will begin to show good growth as the days get warmer.
MAY-JUNE	Blooms appear on the spikes well above the clumps of dark green lance- shaped leaves. Clusters of flowers are borne on spikes.
JULY-AUGUST	Blooming is over, but the plant continues to grow for a while. Sunny locations and some drought are no problem to this plant.
SEPTEMBER	Normal maintenance now as the dormant season approaches. Keep the beds free from weeds.
OCTOBER-NOVEMBER	An occasional flower is not uncommon from the plant, though it is dormant for the most part. Avoid cultivating around the roots of speedwell.
DECEMBER	As winter freezes or frosts cover the area, speedwell becomes dormant in the garden. Mark the bed with a tell-tag so you'll know where your plants are located.

LAWNGRASSES FOR OUR AREA

Growing the Warm Season Grasses

Horticulturists and turf specialists have divided lawn grasses into two groups — warm season and cool season grasses. Folks who have moved to the coastal South from northern areas are probably very familiar with cool season grasses like fescue and Kentucky bluegrass. But the farther South you live, the more you will find warm season grasses as your only choice for a fine lawn. And that may not be a problem, because warm season grasses can be quite handsome, even more so than their northern cousins. For one thing, warm season lawns stay green in the heat of the summer, which is often not the case in cooler areas. Our grasses here along the coast get a good workout because the season that promotes outdoor activity is also the season our lawns are in full growth. This means we have to pay special attention to the maintenance requirements of the grasses we plant.

It is unfortunate that lawns seem to be the standard by which we measure a quality landscape. In an area that offers so many recreational opportunities, our goal should be to spend as little time as possible on the lawn. But this goal isn't always achieved because so many of us place a premium on our turf's appearance. Whether we choose to simply maintain our lawns as easily as possible, or cultivate very fine attractive lawns, most of us spend too much time worrying about them and too much time and effort maintaining them. A recent survey indicated that dandelions and common wood sorrell were present in about ninety percent of coastal lawns, and that homeowners were concerned enough about these two weeds that they wanted to eliminate them at nearly any cost. Yet, most folks are unable to identify them in their neighbors' lawns. When mowed closely enough, most people don't realize there are weeds in the lawn.

As we move into a new era of environmental concern — an era that calls for less fertilization and less use of pesticides — it should be a relief to most folks that lawn care maintenance will take on a decreased emphasis. This is good news for people who wish to enjoy the advantages of a long warm season of recreation and less time caring for lawn grasses.

A good indication that this trend is catching on is the use of more ornamental flower beds and natural areas. Smaller home lots also mean less turf. We can all cut the time we spend on the lawn by planting less of it, and incorporating more flower beds and natural areas in the landscape areas around our homes.

If you are choosing a lawn for your home, replacing an existing turf or renovating the lawn, you'll find the choices are actually few. There are only seven types of warm season grasses that are recommended for our area. In the following guides, you'll find the advantages of each, the care requirements and the best way to keep a premium appearance for you and your neighbors throughout the year.

Jack Davis

Paspalum notatum

Bahiagrass

You'll quickly recognize this grass as the industrial strength grass of highway right-of-ways, parking lots and ball fields. It throws a seed-head very quickly that extends on a long spike with two black-seeded wings. It is a tough, durable grass that resists drought, pests and poor soil. It requires little if any fertilization, and has a very extensive root system that reaches deep into the soil. The leaves are tough and coarse, so it's a bit hard to mow. Not very pleasant to walk on, it is not a premium lawn grass because it is so rough. It does not tolerate shade very well, but thrives in open, hot, sunny locations. If you don't mind cutting it every week, this grass will offer a dense, thick carpet that resists wear and nearly everything that nature or man can toss its way. 'Pensacola' is an old favorite cultivar, but 'Argentine' is preferred for homeowners. You can start this grass from seed, and the cost is minimal.

Grow bahiagrass only if you want durability at the expense of weekly mowing and slightly less than premium appearance.

MONTH-BY-MONTH GUIDE FOR BAHIAGRASS

JANUARY — A brown lawn indicates dormancy.

FEBRUARY-MARCH — Do not use herbicides on your bahiagrass lawn. The thickness of the grass will resist most weeds, and most herbicides will damage this lawn.

APRIL — Green color appears as the lawn breaks dormancy. Even though it is drought-resistant, water your lawn during hot, windy or dry conditions. Half an inch every three days or an inch weekly is ideal. Seed heads will appear.

MAY-JUNE — Excellent growth will take place, and your grass will need to be cut often to eliminate the seed heads.

JULY-SEPTEMBER — Keep the grass cut at three inches. Sharpen the blades of your mower or replace them regularly so that you will "cut" the blades rather than "tear" them. You can collect the clippings, or leave them on the lawn if you have a mulching mower deck.

OCTOBER-NOVEMBER   Bahiagrass goes into dormancy slightly later than other grasses; in fact, cooler weather may cause more aggressive growth. By Thanksgiving, your lawn will start to show some brown patches as lower light triggers dormancy. Keep the lawn cut at three inches.

DECEMBER   Dormacy arrives, but some protected places may be slightly green until a severe cold snap.

Axonopus affinis

Carpetgrass

This coarse grass is perfect for patching or repairing some sections of your lawn that are sparse or need renovation. Similar in growth habit to Saint Augustine, it has the cultural habits of centipedegrass. Carpet has seedheads similar to bahiagrass, and it is not considered a premium lawn. But it does have the advantage of growing in very poor soils, especially those that are very wet. You should use carpet as a patcher or repairer only, not as a main lawn grass, unless you care little for the appearance and wish only to have a maintenance-free lawn. The culture is the same as bahiagrass, and like bahia, it does not perform well in shade.

Eremochloa ophiuroides

Centipedegrass

Perhaps the most popular of the warm season grasses, this is the one that NC State recommends for coastal lawns. Tough, durable and pest-resistant, it is a premium turf. It makes an excellent lawn for pets, children, recreational activities and sports. It doesn't grow well in shade, but it takes the summer sun and heat with ease, and provides wonderful, apple-green coverage over a long season. It greens up quickly in the spring and stays green over a long season, well into October.

You can grow it from seed, sod or plugs, and it "runs" quickly over bare soil, often covering a site in one growing season. It is what we call a "stoloniferous" grass in that it spreads by above-ground stems called stolons. It is susceptible to a pest called ground pearl, an insect for which there is no known cure. Despite this drawback, it remains the favorite lawn grass of the area. Grow centipedegrass with confidence. It will provide you with an excellent, superior lawn for many years without a great deal of maintenance and fertilization.

MONTH -BY- MONTH GUIDE FOR CENTIPEDEGRASS

JANUARY	Your lawn is dormant.
FEBRUARY-MARCH	Some old-timers burn their lawns during this period, but this accomplishes little. So, my advice is: don't bother burning the lawn. Water the lawn at the rate of one half-inch every three days. Late in March, mow the lawn and collect the clippings. If you are using a lawn herbicide, now is the best time to apply it.
APRIL	Around the fifteenth of the month, fertilize with Centipede Plus Brand With Iron fertilizer at the recommended rate. Continue to water the lawn at the rate of one inch weekly. You'll notice some quick green-up as spring approaches. You may need to mow some of the more aggressive sections of the lawn.
MAY	Mow the lawn to two-and-a-half inches. Leave the clippings if you have a mulching deck, and keep the water levels steady at half an inch every three days. No more fertilizers will be needed 'til fall, if you are using the Centipede Plus Brand. This variety of grass is slightly tough, so keep the blades sharp. Remember that dull blades tear the grass rather than cut it.
JUNE-AUGUST	Keep the grass mowed at regular intervals. Water is essential, but don't overwater it. Too much water can be as bad as not enough. If you notice insects and diseases, apply a lawn grass pesticide as needed, following the label instructions carefully. Do not use a chemical pesticide unless you need one. Late in August, get a soil test to determine the pH. Amend the soil accordingly.
SEPTEMBER	Around Labor Day, make another application of Centipede Plus fertilizer. Continue to water and mow as you did during the summer months. This is the last month of the year you can safely purchase sod for repairing and patching.

OCTOBER-NOVEMBER   You might notice some dormancy now as fall approaches. Mowing will become less of a chore. Allow the grass to grow to two-and-a-half inches before cutting.

DECEMBER   By this time, the grass will have "gone to sleep." Dormancy is indicated by a brown lawn.

Stenotaphrum secundatum

St. Augustinegrass

This is the grass of choice for homeowners who want a deep green lawn. Unlike some other grasses which are pale green by nature, St. Augustine is deep green, offering a richer carpet than many other warm season grasses. The blades are slightly wider than centipede, and the grass may be a little thicker, though not quite as dense as centipede. It greens up quicker in the spring and goes into dormancy a little later than many other warm season grasses. It grows in shaded areas, will tolerate drought and pests and is an excellent choice for pets, children and outdoor activities.

St. Augustine is a low-maintenance grass, requires little feeding and is pest-resistant. Though it needs watering regularly, it does not suffer if it doesn't get everything it needs. It will respond quickly to fertilization. The main pests that affect it are brown patch (a fungus that yellows the leaves and fades the grass in widening circles), and chinchbugs and mole crickets which eat the leaves of the grass and destroy large strips of lawns until they are brought into control with lawn pesticides. Some varieties like 'Floratam' are not cold hardy and tend to suffer in colder winters, but 'Raleigh' and 'Seville' are good choices for the coastal area, because they are cold hardy and have a finer textured blade.

St. Augustinegrass is a fine lawn. Not as common as centipede and not recommended as often as some varieties, it will give you everything that you want in a rich, dark green turf, and can be the envy of the neighborhood when kept in good condition. Grow St. Augustine for a wonderful appearance and a lawn that will remind you of the warm season, deep green lawns of the old South.

MONTH-BY-MONTH GUIDE FOR ST. AUGUSTINEGRASS

JANUARY — Your lawn is dormant. Notice a brown grass that looks completely "dead" and has no signs of life.

FEBRUARY — Late this month, apply a pre-emergent herbicide for weed control. You might see some winter hardy weeds like pennywort and Florida betony.

MARCH — Some sections of the lawn that are protected may be green, but the lawn will stay brown with weeds appearing more frequently. If you have not applied a weed killer, now is a good time to do so. Make sure the lawn is watered every three days at the rate of half an inch, and rake the lawn or mow it to keep it clean.

APRIL — Around the fifteenth of the month, make one application of 5-10-30 fertilizer at the recommended rate. Water the lawn, but do not apply any herbicides. You'll see some signs of the lawn breaking dormancy as spring approaches.

MAY-JUNE — Make sure the lawn is watered at the rate of half an inch every three days or one inch weekly. Cut the grass at three inches. Watch for insects and disease which can attack the lawn at any time. Keep the pesticides handy. Make a single application of 16-4-8 timed-release fertilizer at the recommended rates. Get the soil tested and amend accordingly.

JULY-SEPTEMBER — Regular maintenance now as the summer season progresses. Don't let the lawn dry out, but avoid wet conditions, especially at night. Mow the lawn at three inches. Around Labor Day, make a single application of 5-10-30 fertilizer. The lawn will need the same amount of water as in the summer, but wet conditions will enhance fungal growth so keep an eye out for fungal growth and treat as needed.

OCTOBER — Keep the lawn mowed at three inches. Notice some signs of dormancy as some sections of the lawn turn a brown color.

NOVEMBER-DECEMBER — As fall approaches, dormancy sets in, and most of the lawn will turn to a tan color. By Christmas, the lawn will be entirely brown and at this point will be dormant.

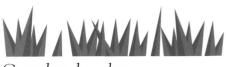

Cynodon dactylon

Common Bermudagrass

This is perhaps the most widely seen lawn grass in the South. In many cases because of its aggressiveness, it is considered invasive. When well-established, common bermuda will run into flower beds, ornamental sections of the garden and even into vegetable gardens. Many people consider this grass to be a weed, and try to eliminate it from their lawns. But it does have advantages. It can be seeded very easily. It grows quickly, requires little care, and if you keep it trimmed, common bermuda can establish a thick lawn in a single growing season. It will not tolerate the slightest shaded area, so if you don't have bright, sunny lawn areas, forget common bermuda.

It is a good idea to see this grass growing in residential areas before you decide to plant it for your lawn, because you may not like it. But in many areas, common bermuda out-performs all the other turf grasses, and with little maintenance, it can provide an excellent coastal Southern lawn. It's pest-free and resistant to many problems that face other premium grasses.

The month-by-month care for common bermudagrass is the same as for hybrid bermuda grass.

Cynodon sp

Hybrid Bermudagrass

There have been some dramatic improvements in bermuda, and these are mostly noted in the golf course grasses we see so often in the South. The 'Tif' series of hybrid bermudas and 'Santa Ana' have proven to be wonderful coastal lawns. These grasses have finer texture and better color than common bermudagrass, and though they require more maintenance, they are often the stars among the fine lawns. Like common bermuda, they will not tolerate shade, but in open, sunny spots, they provide rich, deep green, fine-textured lawns that resemble the famous putting greens and fairways of premium golf courses. You'll need to fertilize them often to keep them in good shape, and it's important to keep them well-watered and weed-free. But once established, these grasses will give you many years of wonderful turf. It's best to cut them with a reel-type mower, because rotary mowers don't seem to mow them close or fine enough to preserve their character. You'll also need to tend them more often than other warm season grasses. But the results are worth the trouble, because hybrid bermuda lawns are some of the finest in the South. Drought-resistant and pest-free, they are wonderful for outdoor activities, children and pets.

MONTH-BY-MONTH GUIDE FOR HYBRID BERMUDAGRASS LAWNS

JANUARY-FEBRUARY   Your lawn is dormant. Notice a very fine, brown turf. Even protected areas are completely brown.

MARCH   Very early in the month, you can use a pre-emergent herbicide to control weeds before they spring up. Be sure that you use a weed killer that is approved for use on bermudagrass, and that the grass is in total dormancy. Once you notice green grass in the lawn, any herbicide may cause damage. Be careful!

APRIL   Around the middle of the month, fertilize the lawn with a single application of 5-10-30 fertilizer at the recommended rate. Water the lawn at the rate of half an inch every three days, and mow it down to one-and-a-half inches, collecting the clippings and debris.

MAY   Around the twentieth of the month, fertilize the lawn with a single application of 16-4-8 timed-release fertilizer at the recommended rate. Maintain the watering level, but make sure the lawn does not stand in water.

JUNE-AUGUST   Keep the grass mowed with a reel-type mower at no more than two inches, but try to maintain a slightly lower height. Insects and disease should not be a problem, but keep the insecticides and fungicides handy in case of attacks. If you notice a problem, solve it quickly and efficiently. Water is essential. Brown areas in the lawn caused by drought will revive quickly, but avoid spending time repairing sections of your lawn.

SEPTEMBER   If you notice areas that need some fertilization, you can apply some 5-10-10 to green up selected sections. Keep a watchful eye out for insects and disease.

OCTOBER   No later than the tenth of the month, make one application of 5-10-30 fertilizer.

NOVEMBER   Your lawn will lapse into dormancy quickly as the fall season approaches. Maintain regular cutting, and do not apply weed killers or fertilizers.

DECEMBER   Dormancy comes quickly in the early days of the month. You'll see a brown lawn develop rapidly in cool weather.

Zoysia matrella

Zoysiagrass

Until a few years ago, zoysia was available only as a sod or sprigged lawn. The two most popular varieties are 'Emerald' and 'Meyer' ('Z-52'). Recently, a seeded selection, 'Sunrise,' has shown some promise as a fine-textured zoysiagrass.

Introduced to the South in the late 1950s, zoysiagrass was supposed to be the greatest innovation in warm season grasses since centipede. But it was expensive and hard to mow, so it never quite caught on as the South's premier turf. Yet, today, it is considered to be the ace of warm season turfs, providing nearly every advantage that a homeowner could want in a fine lawn. It's thick and rich, dark green in color, and wonderful for barefoot walking. It is drought-resistant and has very few pest problems.

It's best to cut this grass with a reel-type mower because of its thick texture. The finer-textured varieties should be kept cut close, at an inch and a half, but the taller varieties,'Meyer's' and 'Sunrise' can be cut at two inches. Water at the usual rate for warm season lawns, an inch and a half every three days.

Zoysia will tolerate some light shade, will resist weeds and pests and will spread quickly. The main disadvantage is that zoysia will drop into dormancy as early as October, and will not green-up in the spring until late April.

But despite staying brown lawn a little longer than other grasses, zoysia will be a premium turf, and will provide a very nice, high quality lawn for your home, your children and pets.

MONTH-BY-MONTH GUIDE FOR ZOYSIAGRASS

JANUARY

Your lawn is dormant.

FEBRUARY-MARCH

Dormancy continues. Late in this period, consider a pre-emergent herbicide that will eliminate any weeds that appear in spring. Use a weed killer that is approved for use on dormant zoysia. Using herbicides once your grass shows green blades can be harmful, so make sure the lawn is completely dormant. Keep the dormant lawn clean of debris.

APRIL

Other warm season grasses may break dormancy during the early days of the month, but zoysia remains brown. Toward the end of the month, make a single application of 5-10-30 fertilizer at the recommended rate.

MAY

On the thirtieth of the month, feed the lawn with a single application of 16-4-8 timed-release fertilizer at the recommended rate. Mow the lawn at the recommended height and leave the clippings on the lawn. Water at the rate of half an inch every three days up to one inch weekly.

JUNE

Your lawn has completely broken dormancy now and will begin to expand rapidly. Normal maintenance now as the season for growth gets underway.

JULY-SEPTEMBER

Weeds and pests will not be a problem if the lawn is well-kept. If it is not green enough to suit you, supplement the earlier feeding with some 5-10-10 fertilizer applied at the recommended rate.

OCTOBER

On the first day of the month, feed the lawn with a single application of 5-10-30 fertilizer. Maintain the grass at the recommended levels for water and mowing.

NOVEMBER-DECEMBER

Dormancy begins earlier than most lawns. Your lawn will be totally brown by Thanksgiving. Once it has turned brown, store the mower and cease maintaining the turf.

Lolium multiflorum

Annual Ryegrass

There is an alternative to a brown, dormant lawn. It's called annual rye or Italian ryegrass and simply "rye" by most coastal Southerners, and it offers a deep green, dense carpet of turf during the winter months when the lawn is otherwise brown. The heat of the late spring and early summer will kill this grass, so it is used only in the fall and winter.

Spread by seed over the existing lawn, the process is called "over-seeding". Usually done at the rate of six pounds per thousand square feet, the seeds of ryegrass germinate directly over the main turf, set roots directly into the lawn and grow in the same soil as the main lawn grass.

Many horticulturists do not recommend using ryegrass every season, because it stimulates your main lawn at a time when it should be dormant, thus causing it to perform at levels it really can't meet. This is due to the fertilizer that you apply to a ryegrass lawn, because without feeding it, rye will not produce the color and texture that you expect in a lawn grass.

But the advantages are obvious. At a time when all else in the landscape is asleep, your lawn will be a vibrant green color, and the smell of freshly cut grass on a winter day is a wonderful break from the dreariness of the cold season. Weigh the advantages of a green grass in winter carefully. You may decide that every third year or so is a good way to enjoy the advantages of a cool season green lawn. In any event, you'll find annual ryegrass to be a wonderful lawn, pest-free and rich in color and texture. You'll have to maintain it carefully, cutting it at three inches every ten days or so, and watering is the same as during the summer months. Fertilize at the rate of ten pounds of actual nitrogen per thousand square feet every six weeks during the growing season.

MONTH-BY-MONTH GUIDE FOR ANNUAL RYEGRASS

JANUARY
The lawn is in full production. Notice a rich green color, except during periods of extreme cold and windy weather. Toward the end of the month, fertilize with 5-10-10 at the rate of twenty pounds per thousand square feet. Water the lawn every three days or so at the rate of half an inch. Cut the grass to three inches in height.

FEBRUARY
Normal maintenance through the month. Avoid fertilizers.

MARCH

Normal maintenance. Keep your mower blades sharp, as dull blades will tear the grass rather than cutting it. Toward the end of the month fertilize again if needed, following the same measures used in January.

APRIL-MAY

Some sections of the grass will develop thick, course clumps of ryegrass. As the heat develops, patches of lawn will die. Avoid all fertilizers and water the lawn as you would for your main season grass.

JUNE

As summer approaches, the ryegrass you seeded will die completely.

JULY-SEPTEMBER

Annual ryegrass will not germinate or survive in the heat of summer.

OCTOBER-NOVEMBER

This is the season for seeding annual ryegrass over the existing lawns. Sow it at the rate of six pounds per thousand square feet and water immediately after seeding. Do not fertilize until the grass has been cut for the first time. Mow at three inches tall.

DECEMBER

Your annual rye is thriving now as the winter season comes in. Fertilize with 5-10-10 at the recommended rate after you cut the lawn for the first time.